The Weeping Child

Andrew A. Ovienloba

Primus International Network for Education and

Developments (PINED)

New York, U.S.A.

Book covers design by lulu .com

Published by Primus International Network for Education and Developments (PINED)

New York, U.S.A.

Printed in the United States of America

Library of Congress Cataloging-in-Publication Data

Ovienloba Andrew A

The Weeping Child

ISBN: 978-0-6151-5871-6

Dedication

This work was published in honor of my Teachers, especially:

1. Mrs. Oyeyemi (1977/78- Army children School Bukuru, Plateau State, Nigeria).

2. Mr. Friday Ukpebor (1980/81- Eguare Primary School, Ewatto, Edo State, Nigeria).

CONTENTS

Forward

Corruption in Nigeria as it is in other nations facing the humiliating challenges of its evil is a topical burning issue. Aside its dysfunctionality to any developmental process, its associative moral odium has particularly compounded Nigeria's image problem both domestically and internationally. Predictably, this has elicited profound intellectual discourse of the corruption problematic

"The Weeping Child" is a book whose critical intervention is anchored on theological insights and thus represents a methodological departure from currents of analysis rooted in secular exposition of the subject matter. The author brings the wisdom of the Catholic Social Teaching that spans beyond a hundred years to focus on the problem of endemic corruption in Nigeria. This peculiarly relative touch is especially assessed across the pages of the book. The topical concept definitions offered arising from his intelligent social analysis of the subject, is particularly insightful and a compelling instrument for both academic resource and a social tool for advocacy.

The new perspective that the author brings to solving the endemic problem of corruption in Nigeria is a perspective of inclusive education that will positively impact the socio political landscape of Nigerian; if the suggestions enshrined in this rare book are critically appreciated. The author's treatment of the subject matter from a historico-analytical method while using the social theological tools of analysis brings to the subject, a new and overwhelming insight that is often treated with an oversight or absolute neglect.

His passion for the subject pulls the reader along in a way that is both entertaining and deeply informative, such that by the end of discuss, the determination for action becomes excruciatingly challenging. The solidity of this work creates and sustains the overriding intention of a social theology in the service of the people.

This is a book that has the potentials of radically affecting the social economic structure of both Nigeria and other nations with the challenges of endemic corruption. The book offers erudite recommendations that have the potentials of re-writing the inglorious history of corruption in Nigeria and other Nations with similar fate. I recommend this book to all who hope and wish for a new world order even beyond the frontiers of Nigeria within both the academia, and advocacy groups. *Transparency International* will find the resources in this book very handy.

John Andrews
Lagos, Nigeria

Acknowledgements

In this edition of my book: **"The Weeping Child**;" I owe unalloyed appreciation to a host of persons who in different ways and at different times contributed towards the realization of this dream.

The contributions of Dr. Harod Horell of the Fordham University New York, USA, to this work is incalculable as he was a pillar in ensuring that the standardization of this social academic contribution is maintained, when I offered it initially as my Master of Arts degree thesis. I pay tribute to all my professors at the Fordham University, Bronx, New York for their contributions towards my intellectual development.

I acknowledge the contribution of the Acton Institute, Oregon, for the fellowship offered towards the initial realization of this project and the various authors whose material and ideas were used in this book.

There are a few other persons whose love, friendship and inspiration I cannot but acknowledge for being a backbone to me in all my endeavors. As these persons are far too numerous to name in this single book without leaving out some persons of great and significant importance, permit me althesame, without meaning any form of individual minimalization to single out Msgr. Robert Trainor, Frs. Thomas Yakubu Gowon Salami, Ambrose Alumiasunya, Daniel Akhimien Ewah, Stephen Ogumah, Joseph Okojie, Egunjobi Pius,

Mrs. Elizabeth Enakhimion, Ms. Bridget Osaguona, and all my Nigeria comrades, for being uniquely what they are to me in this endeavor.

And For all others not mentioned here including members of my family, their contributions are not by any means undermined or minimized; they are valued as gold. May God abundantly bless you all.

Andrew Ovienloba

Author

Preface

Unearthing the Patterns

In his book "Social Ministry" Dicter T. Hessel says: *"the times perplex and unnerve us, our institutions frustrate and immobilize more often than they respond to deepening crisis."* Although Hessel is writing from a North American perspective, his words describe well the contemporary situation in Nigeria.

Nigeria gained her independence from her British colonial master on October 1, 1960; was admitted into the United Nations as member country on October 7, 1960, and held its first democratic elections in 1963. Hence, Nigeria is about forty five years old as an independent nation. The country is also the most populated black or African nation in the world. Still, Nigeria's resources have not been used to benefit the country and its political, social, economic, and, cultural infrastructure, remain largely undeveloped.

One of the greatest problems in Nigeria is that of endemic corruption that has eaten into the fabric of the nation. More fully, corruption has undermined development in Nigeria. The economy has been poorly managed and mismanaged as the common good of the nation has been neglected and those with political influence have used their power for personal gain. Moreover, the youth and young adults of Nigeria have been very negatively affected as their prospects for education and employment have been diminished because of corruption. Overall, the problem of corruption and the effects of corruption on the internal health of the county and the countries external relations with other nations and the broader world must be addressed if Nigeria is to move forward.

This book will provide a theological analysis of the perplexing problem of corruption in Nigeria, a problem that has defied socio-political examinations throughout our political history.   I am concerned with the church as a *"public church"* in the language of Martin Marty and with what Michael J. Himes and Kenneth R. Himes, O.F.M. have called the public significance of theology. As the brothers Himes explain: "What unites those who belong to the public church is the desire to move religious belief away from a narrow concern with personal life which effectively has undercut the church's mission to the wider realm of social existence."[1]

Through my analysis I will show how Christian religious education that fosters an understanding of justice that is grounded within Christian, and especially Catholic, faith traditions can help to address the problem of corruption and ultimately help to heal the wounds caused by the mismanagement of the nation's resources.

What is needed in Nigeria today is a new awareness informed by a conscientious education. According to John Dewey, "democracy

---

[1] Michael J. Himes et al; Fullness of Faith: The Public Significance of Theology (New York, Paulist Press 1993)p.1

has to be born anew every generation, and education is its midwife."
If this claim by John Dewey is anything to go by, then what we need
in Nigeria is a rebirth of democracy that can only be arrived at
through a directed education. This is the kind of education that will
not only affect the conscience of Nigerians, but that will spark a
process of change that will take generations to complete.

My endeavor in this book is to use the wealth of Catholicism
to provide a pastoral resource that can help to heal Nigeria's endemic
problem of corruption. My strategic goal is to package an educational
curriculum or program that could be used for religio-civic education
in Nigeria and that will positively empower the people to recognize
how Christian faith can serve as a rich resource for addressing the
perplexing problem of endemic corruption.

To address the issue of corruption in Nigeria is to raises
questions about socio-economic and political morality. Moreover, the
social evils caused by corruption have led to perpetual humiliation of
the poor and vulnerable, those who live on the margins of Nigerian
society. A discussion of corruption in Nigeria must, in order to be
complete, address the plight of the poor and most vulnerable citizens
of this country.

In this work, I will make use of the model of social analysis
developed by Joc Holland and Peter Henriot in an "effort to obtain a
more complete picture of a social situation by exploring its historical

and structural relationships,"[2] specifically the social situation caused by endemic corruption in Nigeria. I will begin by inserting myself in the social context of Nigeria and excavating the root causes of corruption in Nigeria, its structure, dynamics and growth in the social main stream, including the values encouraging the social malaise over the years.

After tracing analytically the root causes and effects of corruption in Nigeria, as in its thesis and antithesis, (that is, understanding the corruption problem as an historical form of consciousness that contains within itself incompleteness that gives rise to opposition, or a conflicting concept or form of consciousness[3]), I will then offer a theological analysis of the problem based upon an understanding of principles of justice developed as part of the tradition of modern Catholic social teaching. I will emphasize how these principles of justice can be used to empower the people, especially the poor and most vulnerable, to address the identified problem of endemic corruption in the aforementioned society. I will also show how principles of justice can serve as a pastoral resource and be incorporated into pastoral programs that can be used in religious education in Nigeria to address the issue of endemic corruption.

---

[2] Joe Holland et al; Social Analysis Linking Faith and Justice (New York, Dove Communications and Orbis Books, 2004)p98
[3] Microsoft® Encarta® Reference Library 2002. © 1993-2001 Microsoft Corporation. All rights reserved: George Wilhelm Frederick Hegel. "Dialectics"

The work will be divided into four interrelated chapters including the preface. The chapters will further be subdivided into subsections for the sake of the logical coherence of ideas. The preface chapter, this introductory chapter presents the problem of endemic corruption and outlines how I offer a theological and religious educational analysis of this problem.

Chapter one is entitled "*A Historical Overview of the Problem of Corruption in Nigeria.*" I will explore the history and demographic structure of Nigeria as a people and as a country. In the sections of the chapter I am analyzing Nigeria's cultural character or heritage, social stratifications/socio-economic profile, dominant social problems and the country's past attempts to resolve its social problem of endemic corruption.

In chapter two, having already identified the Nigerian social problem of endemic corruption in the previous chapter, I am looking at "*The Justice Implications of Corruption in Nigeria.*" The trend of thought is principally to look at the antithesis or opposing historical consciousness of the problem of endemic corruption in Nigeria. More fully, I will examine the social and economic effects of the endemic problem of corruption on the entire social polity, focusing on the culture of lawlessness that has been a product of endemic corruption in the society. The chapter highlights the sad effects of corruption on the socio-economic and political health of the country and how these have led to increasing efforts to resolve the problem of corruption.

The focus of the third chapter is on the presentation of *"A Catholic Theological Principle of Justice."* Faith in the inalienable dignity of the human person as a social being - as seen in the light of Christian scripture, especially the passages in which Jesus teaches that the moral law can be summarized by the command to love God and one's neighbor – is the cornerstone of all Catholic moral teaching. This chapter, divided into five sub-sections, is an attempt to situate the problem of endemic corruption in Nigeria within the social teachings of the Catholic Church. Beginning with an understanding of the dignity of the human person, I focus specifically on the theological principles of justice as essential for securing and safeguarding the rights of persons and on the preferential option for the poor as a way to measure how well a society fosters respect for persons.

The fourth and concluding chapter is my contribution to the field of knowledge, since it contains my suggested program for addressing the named endemic social malaise. Thus, it is entitled *"Solving the Nigerian Endemic Corruption Equation."* The intention in this chapter is to challenge the Nigerian ecclesiastical hierarchy to take the initiative in the fight against corruption in Nigeria. In proposing this challenge various documents of the church as a universal community are explored to demonstrate why the onus lies with the church to take the lead. Moreover, the chapter also takes a bold step in outlining a systemic program of activities that can be utilized for the national battle of social purgation of the problem of endemic corruption in Nigeria. The strategic approach offered in this last chapter is a process of directed pastoral religious education for use in schools and parish settings.

Andrew A. Ovienloba

Author

Chapter One

An Historical Overview of the Problem of Endemic Corruption in Nigeria

"The attempt to be free of the past is an unworthy illusion and

To be free of the future a dangerous mistake....People will not look

forward to prosperity who will not look backward to their ancestors"

Himes and Himes, 1993

1.0   Introduction

Nigeria as a people came under the British colonial rule in 1906.[4] Prior to this experience, the country that is now Nigeria was as a number of independent kingdoms and States. The concept of a country called Nigeria came into existence with the amalgamation edit of 1914 under the leadership of Lord Lugard, the British designated Governor General of Nigeria at the time. The amalgamation was a coming together of convenience for the advantage of the British government. In other words there was no universal decision on the part of the different kingdoms or vassal states for a merger. The name Nigeria was derived by Lord Lugard's

---

[4] Microsoft Encarta Reference Library 2002 (1993-2001 Microsoft Corporation -Nigeria)

colonial administration from one of the major rivers in Nigeria, called "River Niger".

Nigeria as a country gained her independence from her British colonial master and became a member of the Commonwealth of Nations on October 1st 1960. She became a member of the United Nations on October 7, 1960. Nigeria as it exists today has a population estimated to be about 150 million people with about 250 languages or ethnic groupings.[5] There are three major religious groupings in the country: Christianity, Islam and African Traditional religion. Nigeria is the largest and most populous country in Africa. She is richly endowed with abundant natural and human resources. "Iron-ore deposits are widespread in the savannah region of Nigeria, as are salt deposits. Tin and columbite are found in the plateau area. Great deposits of petroleum and natural gas are located in the Niger delta and offshore in the bights of Benin and Bonny of the Gulf of Guinea. Nigeria, also, has large deposits of coal, lead, and zinc, and small deposits of gold and uranium."[6]

If Nigeria has all the above enumerated qualities of natural and human endowment, then why and where does the question of corruption/poverty prevail?

---

5 Www. Nigeria. COM
6 Microsoft Encarta Reference Library 2002 op. cit (Nigeria)

1.1 Origin and Dynamics of Corruption in Nigeria

The Collins dictionary defines corrupt/corruption as lacking in integrity, open to or involving bribery or moral perversion, and dishonesty. The Cambridge dictionary (online) gives the meaning of the adjective "corrupt" as: "dishonestly using your position or power to your own advantage, especially for money." In defining the noun "corruption" it indicates clearly that it is something morally bad. The Oxford pocket dictionary defines corrupt as: "made unreliable by errors or alterations", or as "dishonest especially using bribery." These definitions make it clear that corruption has to do with the perversion or distortion of some form of relationship or contract. In this study, corruption will be considered as an abuse of power within the political order or within a given circle of trust involving political leadership and power.

Corruption and good governance are interrelated subjects. The absence of good governance creates administrative pollution that is capable of raising myriads of problems in any organizational structure. Such problems could include; corruption, poverty, unnecessary delay in service delivery to the people and a protracted hindrance in the development of a nation. According to Wangari Maathai,

Corruption is a universal phenomenon but, just like other global crimes against humanity, such as the slave trade and colonialism, corruption bothers our conscience so much because it is a business extra-ordinary, without mercy or compassion. It thrives because it pays good dividends at whichever level the investment is made.[7]

For him again, "Colonialism and corruption were inseparable. When the colonial administration and indeed even the missionaries arrived, they used a form of corruption to get corroborators and converts."[8] Thus the problem of corruption in Nigeria, as it may be with all other post colonial African countries, has its roots in the colonial experience. As a matter of historical fact,

the origins of many of the problems afflicting Nigerian society can be traced back to the colonial era. It was only at the beginning of the twentieth century that Britain formally brought the territory to become known as Nigeria under full colonial control; but a British presence in the region had been there centuries before, initially conflicting with Portuguese and French interests, and then surpassing them. Nigeria made little sense as a country except to imperial mapmakers. The country was grabbed in the wholesale 'Scramble for Africa' at

---

[7] Maathai, Wangari. Developing Anti Corruption Strategies in a Changing World: Global Challenges to Civil Society. (www. Transparency.org / 9th international Anti-corruption conference, The Papers)
[8] Ibid.

the end of the nineteenth century, when British forces amalgamated many diverse ethnic and religious groups into the new colonial state. The convenient policy of "indirect rule" offered a limited form of autonomy for each region (particularly in the north), though always within the overriding constraints of colonial rule. [9]

Additionally,

Modern African states [like Nigeria] were [equally] born out of colonial systems which were based on corruption, nurtured by institutions which violated human rights and thrived because of inequalities and injustices. The states were indeed handed down to ruling elite who had been trained into the same school of thought and who shared the same values. This ruling class did not have the welfare of all their people at heart. They were more committed to their own interests and that of their partners, whether they were from the West or from the East, North and South. We even fought bitter wars over which friend to adopt. [10]

---

9. Stephen Wright, *Nigeria: Struggle for Stability and Status* (Boulder, CO: Westview Press, 1998), 1,

[10] Maathai, Wangari. *Developing Anti Corruption Strategies in a Changing World: Global Challenges to Civil Society*. Ibid

This is not to conclude however that all pre-colonial African cultures were absolutely devoid of corruption. The point to be noted instead is that the dynamics of corruption as they exist today developed primarily during the colonial experience. Maathai supports and helps to justify this claim when he states:

> For example, they gave out gifts like blankets, clothing, sugar, salt etc, These were considered good incentives but they were mild forms of bribes and kickbacks to persuade the natives to bend their code of conduct and values, and to agree to a deal which erased any sense of responsibility and accountability, to undermine the community....Those who accepted to be corrupted were later promoted to be the chiefs, we all know that from our history books. By agreeing to become agents used to undermine the freedom of their own communities, they may have lost integrity, but they benefited, and that justified the means. In time, they were doing so well, that they started being looked up to as the models. Those who had stuck to their values and integrity looked so much worse off. They looked rather stupid not to have taken advantage of opportunities presented to them in the new world.[11]

In Nigeria for instance, it is a common knowledge in the history of the Binis that, during the Benin massacre, and the deportation of the Oba of Benin Kingdom, (Oba Ovoramwen

---

[11] Ibid

Nogbaise) to Calabar; that the betrayers of the aforesaid Oba, were some of his trusted chiefs bribed by the British soldiers with dry gins, day guns, and other accessories; just to point out where the Oba was hiding. These chiefs became the quasi Lords of the land after the dethronement of the Oba. This experience was not only a baptism in corruption for the people, but also an unhealthy reversal of the previously held moral laws of the land. Prior to this experience, the traditional culture encouraged the fear of being punished by the gods of the land, should one defraud his/her neighbor.   Precautionary measures were taken based on these ancestral laws of the land to avoid what could possibly bring a curse to the land. Moreover, people who were found guilty of bringing a curse on the land were not only defamed but treated with disdain and levity.

The new system of regionalization and "indirect rule"[12] governance adopted by the colonial masters also intensified the corruption in Nigeria.

---

[12] When British colonial forces finally overcame the Sokoto Caliphate in 1900-1903, the conqueror, Frederick Lugard, recognized the strength and sophistication of the emirate system- in the collection of taxes -and used it as the basis for a form of "indirect rule" (i.e. ruling through the local chiefs) in northern Nigeria. As governor-general of the whole country, Lugard tried to introduce indirect rule into southern Nigeria. In Yorubaland for instance, there were clearly defined states with rulers who could be recognized as Native Authorities. Elsewhere, however, the situation was very different. The large cities and towns of the south had fluid and mixed ethnic structures which made direct rule necessary in the form of European-style municipal authorities. The diffuse and egalitarian society of the south-east provided no obvious traditional rulers. The British tried to impose rulers, for the benefit of their adopted system of tax collection rule, but the results were disastrous. Divisions and hoodwinking or official betrayal for monetary gain enveloped the entire system to the disadvantage of the communities involved. Even

...indirect rule and the creation of distinct regional governments and economies fragmented the embryonic Nigerian unity and established rivalries between ethnic and religious groups that undermined the fragile consensus. The nationalist movement itself, though not national in composition, was a national umbrella for various sub-national groupings. After independence, these built-in tensions mushroomed, contributing to the collapse of the First Republic in 1966 and to the ensuing bloody civil war over Biafran secession. This war cast a shadow over the Nigerian psyche, and its memory perhaps helped to prevent similar secessionary attempts. [13]

In essence this new system led to a strategy of divide and rule. This mode of leadership in the colonial administration of Nigeria brought hoodwinking in different ways just to attract the reward of the colonial masters. In a joint pastoral letter issued by the Nigerian hierarchy on October 1st 1960 among other things, the Bishops observed that:

---

when the British administration eventually agreed to recognize the traditional councils of the region as the Native Authorities for implementing indirect rule, the damage had been done beyond repair; corruption was stamped in high places of power. The pace of corruption in Nigeria today bears eloquent testimony in that direction.

Microsoft® Encarta® Reference Library 2002. © 1993-2001 Microsoft Corporation. All rights reserved.

13. Stephen Wright, *Nigeria: Struggle for Stability and Status. Op Cit.* p. 2.

We are faced, for example, with a widespread dash-bribe system that is slowing up our economy, causing deaths on the roads and impeding efficient administration. We urge the governments to take decisive action in this grave issue. Those in official posts especially must be reminded that men who take bribes betray the trust of the nation. Bribery is a great sin that usually does injury to the poor. [14]

This observation by the Nigeria Bishops at the time authenticates the claim that even within colonial administration there was already widespread bribery and corruption. This evil of corruption was a parting gift from the masters to their disciples who were the ruling elite. If their masters lived a consumptive life that was unquestionable by the poor masses, they too adopted that way of life. Therefore,

to sustain the very consumptive colonial lifestyle, the ruling elite needed a lot of wealth which could not be made without domination and exploitation of the very people they were expected to protect. They therefore, became non-accountable and non-transparent to their citizens. They had to be dictatorial and oppressive. They ignored democratic principles and human rights... Corruption was perceived as an opportunity, a time to accumulate wealth and hide it in some secret accounts

---

[14] Schineller, Peter, ed. The Voice of the Voiceless: Pastoral Letters And Communiqués of the Catholic Bishops' Conference of Nigeria 1960-2002 (Ibadan, Nigeria Daily Graphics Nigeria Limited, 2002)p.11.

in countries which specialized in hiding stolen wealth. Even at the national level, corrupt individuals and their wealth were protected by institutions which should have arrested and prosecuted them.[15]

The evidence of this bad foundation came to light shortly after the independence of Nigeria in 1960. The elections of 1963 were marred by violence and allegation of corruptions, and this then resulted in an unbearable crisis in 1966 as the government became unable to operate effectively. This unwholesome experience led further to the first military coup and eventually to the civil war between 1967 and 1970. The pains and woes of the war brought new challenges that further entrenched corruption and robbery in the society as sad gains of the war. This experience, sad as it is perhaps, is validated by the recent observations of the Norwegian Institute of International Affairs and Maxwell School of Syracuse University when they *"highlighted that geopolitical changes and transformations of the global economy after the Cold War have aggravated the problem of corruption worldwide."*[16]

Today, in Nigeria, after nearly fifty years of Independence, the problem has taken a new and sophisticated shift with different names at different levels of operations. These names include the following: *"kick back", "back rubbing", "hand wetting", "419", "settlement",*

---

[15] Wangari Maathai. Op. Cit
[16] Upadhyay, Dr. Niranjan, Prasad. "The Rising Nepal: Editorial/Opinion: Corrupt Practices Result of Bad Governance." www.gorkhapatra.org.np; p. 3.

"file movement", and so on. Let us at this point examine other causes of corruption in Nigeria before we proceed to explore the different types of corruption evident in the society and the levels on which the different types of corruption operate.

1.2 Other causes of corruption in Nigeria

Cultural expectations: With the growth of the Nigerian polity, certain cultural expectations that were previously based on age and natural bravery have been redefined in terms of economic power. The cultural expectations include, title taking, i.e., a chieftaincy title and the expectations of not just owning a house but an awe inspiring kind of building that will command respect among peer groups. Previously, owning a house was more of a community effort when a man came to an age. The great shift in orientation despite its social advantage came about as a result of destructive acculturation. This is a systemic acculturation that trained the people to imitate the consumptive life style of the colonial masters.

Another cultural expectation today is the strain of extended family care coupled with elaborate marriage ceremonies and funeral rites for deceased parents. The excessive reproductive drive of the people, often tied to a cultural appreciation of child bearing, in many cases overtaxes the meager resources of a family. To make ends meet point, the bread winners of some families relax their moral standard and give in to corruption. According to Victor Dike, the influence or pressure of 'polygamous household' and extended family system, and pressure to meet family obligations, which are more in Less Developed Countries, are some of the causes of corruption. Thus, Merton (1968) acknowledges the relationship between culture and corruption. And Banfield (1958) shows a relationship between corruption and strong family orientation. The study, which helped to explain high levels of corruption in southern Italy and Sicily, shows that "Corruption is linked to the strong family values involving intense feelings of obligation." Lack of effective control and taxing systems are other problems. Thus, Lotterman (April 25, 2002) who noted that bad rules breed corruption, acknowledged that 'ineffective taxing system' makes it difficult for societies to track down people's financial activities.[17]

Moreover, because of the social elevation brought about by the ill-gotten wealth, the corrupt official may be given unbeatable protection by both the family and kindred. He may even be given a chieftaincy title by the community and a title in the church, as if to be confirmed in his/her bravery in the defeat of integrity by corruption.

Socio-economic factors: In the pre-colonial African society any unquestionable wealth attracted concern from members of the

---

[17] Victor E. Dike. Managing the Challenges of Corruption in Nigeria. (*CEO Centre for Social Justice and Human Development (CSJHD), Sacramento, California June, 2003*).

immediate family, and the society at large often suspected that the person was involved in occult practices. Today, wealth is definitely glorified in most circles irrespective of the source(s) of acquisition. Poverty is seen as form of debasement. This, by and large, drives people to enrich themselves by any means. Yes, poverty is indeed an assault on human dignity. However, corruption is a greater moral evil that promotes persistent economic poverty of an even greater number of people.

Socio-economic forces in Nigeria today often exalt the Michael Avellian dictum that might is right. This explains why a lot of people fight, and are ready to die if only to have access to political or military power; not for love of the country so as to gallantly serve the people, but to have a sizeable share of the national cake.

Absence of Functional and Reliable Utilities: The absence of functional and reliable utilities like hospitals, electricity, water supply, telecommunications etc. leads people to exploit dubious means in search of a more desirable and comfortable life. In a situation where the social rights of all have been subordinated to the social privileges of a few, there will be people who seek out and then follow dubious ways of getting ahead in life. The end then justifies the means. If this logic is consistently followed it becomes a confirmation of the Edo adage that states that: *"whatever is used to destroy the enemy does not matter much in so far as it reaches the grave"*. The quest for survival, then, in the absence of any meaningful social structure leads people to exploit the system negatively for their own benefit.

1.3 Types of Corruption in Nigeria

Corruption can be categorized into two regular types in Nigeria; namely: structural and endemic corruption.

➢ Structural or systemic corruption in Nigeria

This is the kind of corruption that exists within government structures. It could also be referred to as bureaucratic corruption. It undermines the democratic dynamics and frustrates the free flow of administrative provisions for development. Those who give into systemic corruption abandon the moral ideal of good governance and frustrate the system for their personal gains and benefits. Service delivery for this kind of corruption is anchored in gratification and extra-financial reward from citizens for government officials, aside from their remuneration. They call this kind of corruption "settlement". This is a systemic defeat of good governance; given the understanding that,

> Good governance always relates with effective delivery of services to the general people. [more so that] in the course of imparting effective services to the citizens, the bureaucrat's behavior should be fair and he or she must possess fundamental characteristics i.e. trust, consistency, integrity,

equitable treatment, sense of ownership, mutual respect and impartial decision making[18]

When systemic corruption permeates a government contracts are awarded based on what the contractor is able to part with rather than competence. This is the kind of corruption called *"kick back."* In this systemic pattern of corruption, responsibility and ownership are abandoned, while development is minimized. On a vertical level, this kind of corruption leads to over centralization of power in the person at the apex of administration so that the person can maximize his or her personal gain. Horizontally, the lower officer maximizes profit from every available opportunity on his/her level in dealing with clients. Service in a systemically corrupt system is usually marred by mediocrity. A boss may employ his family members and associates in important positions of authority irrespective of qualifications.

Success and influence is judged here by the amount of money the individual government official is able to embezzle for his/her self enrichment. He/she is judged not necessarily by the quality of service rendered while in office, but by the number of houses acquired, the quality of the fleet of cars bought as personal gain while in office.[19] Once again the Catholic Bishops' Conference in 1999 challenged this ugly trend in their joint pastoral letter of that year when they declared:

---

[18] Upadhyay, Dr. Niranjan Prasad. Op Cit

[19] This is an emulation of what the earliest followers of the colonial masters were. There is a saying in Nigeria, that you cannot be a faithful servant of the master and remain poor unless you are cursed. In other words if you are trusted by the colonial master, he/she will make you rich by whatever means. There is a National Television program in Nigeria today called "Ichioku" that serves as a satire to that effect.

It is evident that corruption has done incalculable damage to Nigeria and Nigerians. Its effects on the nation have been many, all of them negative. Among other things, it has bred gross inefficiency of public institutions and eroded people's confidence in those institutions, including government and its agencies, parastatals, security organizations, the judiciary, schools, hospitals, to name but a few. Corruption has led to diminished productivity in both the public and private sectors.[20]

According to Olu Olagoke, in his book '*The incorruptible judge*,' "if the citadel of court is corrupt, what will happen to the body polity, it will be completely rotten and collapse." This is the story of our great country called Nigeria. Our rulers and dictators have consistently betrayed us, corrupted our system, and so, Nigerians are vandalized and vanquished morally and economically.

➤ Endemic corruption in Nigeria

For the purpose of this work I would like to classify as endemic corruption all other forms of corrupt practices that exist in Nigerian society. The morale of the common person has been destroyed because of the culture of corruption that flows from all echelons of government. It is almost difficult to know in Nigeria

---

[20] Schineller, Peter, editor. The Voice of the Voiceless. Op. Cit., p.395.

when a demand for service delivered or to be delivered is genuine or dubious. The statement of the Catholic Bishops' Conference of Nigeria on this subject makes it even clearer when they declared that:

> We are painfully aware that corruption has eaten deep into the very fabric of the Nigerian society. It has become so pervasive that many now accept it as the "Nigerian Way of life" or the Nigerian way of doing things. People now speak about a so-called "Nigerian factor", when they mean corruption. The situation is so bad that corruption has been institutionalized to a point where it almost passes for official policy in both the Public and private sectors of our national life. The socio-economic and political system itself appears to be built on corruption and thrives on it.[21]

Indeed, corruption has created deep and undeserved poverty among the vast majority of Nigerians. It is a case of poverty in the midst of affluence. The map attached to this document from Transparency International (see Appendix 1), which described Nigeria as the second most corrupt country in the world, says it all. The entire country is painted black without mercy. This is a call for urgent action.

Furthermore; according to Victor E. Dike (CSJHD), corrupt activities in Nigeria could also include political corruption, bureaucratic corruption, electoral corruption, embezzlement and

---

[21] Ibid p.394

bribery. Political corruption, which takes place at the highest levels of political authority, is a 'corruption of greed.' It affects the manner in which decisions are made, manipulates and distorts political institutions and rules of procedure. Bureaucratic corruption, which occurs 'in the public administration" or 'the implementation end of politics,' is the 'low level' and 'street level' corruption. This is the type of corruption the citizens encounter daily in hospitals, schools, local licensing offices, interaction with the police, taxing offices, etc. It is a petty' -'corruption of need' - that occurs when one obtains services or business permit or permissions from the public sector through inappropriate procedures. Additionally, electoral corruption includes the purchase of votes, promises of office or special favors, coercion, intimidation and interference with the freedom of elections. Corruption in the public offices involves sales of legislative votes, administrative or judicial decisions, or governmental appointment. Other forms of corruption include embezzlement (theft of public resources by public officials) and bribery (i.e. persuading others to act improperly by a gift of money, etc.).

1.4 .The Fight against Corruption in Nigeria down Through the Ages

From the beginning of independent Nigeria, various governments both civilian and military have professed to commit themselves to the fight against corruption in Nigeria. All the military interventions in the civil arena beginning with the one of 1966 under the leadership of late General Johnson Agui-Irosin to the government take -over by late General Sani Abacha have always been presented under the pretext of saving the country from corruption and disintegration.

It suffices to mention here some of the efforts made across the years of Nigerian independence by various governments to rid the country of the sad history of corruption. I will, in order to keep this analysis at a manageable length, limit myself to a review of the most recent efforts. Overall, the fact that corruption continues to be one of the greatest banes of the Nigerian developmental problem in spite of the claimed averred programs, reveals the flaws in such preceding efforts to solve the debacle caused by corruption.

The first concrete historical attempt I will mention here is the *War against indiscipline* (WAI) of General Muhammadu Buhari/ Tunde Idiagbon of 1983. After taking over power through a military coup from the elected government of Alhaji Shehu Shagari, the Buhari government began by calling all elected politicians to account for their ill gotten wealth. This curbed corruption for a while because many people were afraid to violate or oppose the popular WAI program. Unfortunately, it turned out to be the case of the hunter becoming the hunted. The superficial program ended in fiasco because of the lack of a strong will on the part of the government. When the administration was toppled by a General Ibrahim Babaginda led coup in 1985, another effort was commenced. Even though this administration attempted with minimal result to revive the economy, it turned out to be one of the most corrupt regimes in Nigerian political history. Their structural adjustment program (SAP) brought unbearable hardship to Nigerians without evident quantifiable results as gains for the sacrifice made.

The next administration that attempted to tackle the problem of corruption in Nigeria was the despotic regime of General Sani Abacha. He introduced the War against Indiscipline and Corruption (WAIC) while this initiative was announced boldly on bill boards along the highways it was never implemented or put into practice, in line with the widest effective imaginative sense created by the hullabaloo of the roadside billboards, across the length and breadth of Nigeria highways. At best the WAIC turned out to be the foundation stone for the ill fated, ill motivated, self succession bid of the General Sani Abacha as a life president of Nigeria; until the faithful day in June of 1998 when he was arrested by the cold hands of death.   It is of particular importance to note that chief among other factors that accentuated the chronic condition of the economy in Nigeria is the absence of strong political good will. Again we can reference the religio-tribal bigotry and authentic sense of nationalism among those privileged with both military and political power certainly impoverish the struggling economy with the presence lots of people with intelligent self interest at the center of governance.

Furthermore, increasing debt, structural adjustment, decreased foreign investment, rampant corruption, and a soft oil market all were causes, and features, of the poor economy. The failure to implement democratic reforms in the 1990s (especially evident with the annulment of the 1993 presidential election, which brought victory to Chief Moshood Abiola, a Muslim Yoruba) led to some modest sanctions by the Commonwealth, the European Union (EU), and the United States. Although the sanctions themselves were relatively mild, deliberately excluding oil exports, they contributed to the environment of ostracism that weakened Nigeria's economic linkages and undermined its national pride and status. [22]

1.5 The Battle against Corruption in Nigeria under President Olusegun Obasanjo

One of the first public commitments that Chief Olusegun Obasanjo made before the people of Nigeria, millions of whom voted him into office in 1999 with high hopes of reform, was a pledge to rid Nigeria of corruption. He further demonstrated his commitment to this cause by setting up the Independent Corrupt Practices and Other Related Offences commission (ICPC). He equally set up the Economic and Financial Crimes Commission (EFCC). Unfortunately, his first tenure of office as the president (1999-2003) witnessed another trail of corrupt politicians in his cabinet while the ICPC and

---

22. Stephen Wright, *Nigeria: Struggle for Stability and Status* (Boulder, CO: Westview Press, 1998), 3,

EFCC showed themselves to be the giant yet powerless anti-corruption commissions.

In 2001, the FATF (The Financial Action Task Force)[23] woke Nigeria and five other countries up by putting them on its list. Nigeria had a 1995 anti-money-laundering law, but it had never achieved anything. In 2003, Nigeria established the EFCC to fight corruption. The law specifically provided for the Nigerian financial Intelligence Unit (NFIU), a concession by Nigeria to the FATF and the fight against money laundering and financing of terrorism. According to the EFCC, establishing the NFIU was a precondition for the removal of Nigeria from the NCCTs (FATF's list of Non Cooperating Countries or Territories)[24]. Although all of the countries that Nigeria entered the list with four years ago have been removed, Nigeria has not.[25]

---

[23] Financial Action Task Force (FATF) is an inter-governmental body whose purpose is to establish international standards, and develop and promote policies, both at national and international levels, to combat money laundering (ML) and the financing of terrorism (FT).

[24] That is, countries that lack the appropriate restrictions and resources to combat money laundering and terrorism financing. As at October 2005, only three countries are still down on the list, which includes: Myanmar, Nauru and Nigeria. Indonesia, the Philippines and the Cook Islands were the latest jurisdictions to be removed from the list and to get a clean bill of health. **References:** FATF Annual and Overall Review of Non Cooperative Countries or Territories; June 10, 2005; www OECD.com; Larry Johnson, The Counterterrorism Blog: February 14-20, 2005

[25] (Nigerian) *Guardian Newspaper Limited:* Sunday May 1, 2005. – Editorial/Opinion

Still, President Olosegun Obasanjo's recent indictment of two members of his cabinet on grounds of corruption seemed to allow all to breathe a sigh of hope that the government now realizes that governance is the process where by public institutions conduct public affairs, manage public resources and guarantee the realization of human rights. More so, good governance is nothing short of a process that accomplishes the people's hopes and aspiration in an atmosphere free of abuse and corruption. Sonala Olumhese of the *Guardian Newspaper* perhaps put it best when he expressed the hopes of the Nigeria people in the fight against corruption thus:

> as Nigerians, we are hopeful that if our assault on corruption succeeds, we will one day see our beloved country taken off the basement of Transparency International's embarrassing list of the most corrupt. This is why we are happy that the Economic and Financial Crimes Commission (EFCC) has begun to make an impact in putting significant Nigerian names in the same sentence as the term, "corruption charges."[26]

Everyone rejoices to see that even the inspector general of Police (Mr. Tafa Balogun), who is supposed to be the chief law enforcement official against corrupt public and private officials, or the senate president of the federal republic of Nigeria (Chief Adolphus Wabara), can be held accountable for alleged corruption. Yet, a lot of Nigerians are still asking about the fate of the government leaders

---

[26] Ibid

previously accused of mishandling or stealing three hundred million, two hundred million, one hundred million, and eighty two million Naira (N300,000,000.00; N200,000,000.00; N100,000,000.00; N82,000,000.00), respectively, during the 1999-2003 political tenure of office?[27] Many more are beginning to question the sincerity of purpose on the part of President Obasanjo in the fight against corruption in Nigeria. "One would re-call that Chief Obasanjo made a 'financial deal' with the family of Late General Sani Abacha who looted the nation. But he fired Mr. Vincent Azie (the acting Auditor-General) whose audit report indicted the executive, legislative and judiciary branch (among other agencies) for 'improper accounting practices' (See the _Daily Independent_ of Jan 13, 2003 and Feb 26, 2003 and Ugwuanyi, in _Vanguard_ of Feb 21, 2003). The Abacha deal and the Azie's case show that Chief Obasanjo does not have the will to fight corruption in Nigeria;"[28] as was anticipated at the inception of his political administration. His double deal with corrupt state governors to achieve his manipulative bid for a third term in office is nothing but a corrupt attempt to manipulate the cause of justice in Nigeria for his personal advantage.

---

[27] Ovienloba, Andrew, editor. The Social Crusade: Thoughts and Reflections (Benin City, Nigeria JDPC Publications, 2004)p.75 ; Where are the past military Generals who looted and plundered our national account while in office as heads of State, where are our past civilian government officials, Alhaji Umaru Diko, of 1979-83, where are people like of Chris Uba of Anambara etc? How about Sate governors who travel after every federal allocations, while pensions and salaries are unpaid, roads and public schools in disrepair while their children and wards study abroad?
[28] Victor Dike, "Managing the Challenges of Corruption in Nigeria" Op Cit.

Moreover, the problem in Nigeria is not just the administration of justice through the prosecution of the corrupt officials who are out of favor with those in power in the current presidential administration. No, many Nigerians feel that,

> Something is seriously wrong when only the politicians, political office holders, and top public officers constitute the only set of people that can boast of plenty at a time of general want. Nigerians are no fools. No one should expect them to be happy that some people, who are by no means homeless, can dole out N500 million or more just to buy another house. When national lawmakers are awarding themselves jumbo salaries and allowances that enable a senator to go home with N1.3 million every month, workers know that part of that money should have been for their upkeep. It is absurd that the senate president can get N2.1 million a week as overseas travel allowance, at a time the average worker can hardly afford two meals a day, [while a lot of Nigerian university graduates are roaming the streets jobless and almost hopeless].[29]

The superficialities with which this government and past governments seem to have attended to the palpable questions of a corruption that have led the majority of the people to become poor beggars living amidst affluence and opulence in their own motherland, become

---

[29] *Guardian Newspaper* Op Cit. (Sanyaolu Kunle : Working and Suffering)

reasons why a social integration of the Catholic theological principles of justice into the system is essential. However, before we critically assess the possibility of assimilating the Catholic theological principles of justice into the 'socio-surgical' arena of reform, let us first explore some of the justice implications of corruptions in Nigeria. Through such an exploration we can come to appreciate more fully the destructive influence of the evil of corruption in Nigeria as an issue that needs to be addressed by the Church

Chapter Two

The Justice Implications of Corruption in Nigeria

"A just social system is impossible without people being just. Justice is first and foremost a virtue, and it inheres in individuals and institutions that carry out God's commandment to care for one another-to feed the hungry, heal the sick, and enable the able-bodied to work and contribute to the commonweal
- Bellah, et al., The Good society, p.282

2.0 Introduction

When we talk about the justice implications of corruption in Nigeria, we refer to the concrete consequences of the unattended problem of corruption, its long and short term effect on the society both for the present and the future.

Whereas the long and short term implications of the unattended problem of corruption in Nigeria are multifarious, I would like to limit myself to the following points for the sake of emphasis, and elaborate on their present and future consequences for the Nigerian polity.

> **3.1 Hazardous Economic Growth in Nigeria**
> **3.2 Endemic Poverty in Nigeria**
> **3.3 Lawlessness in Nigeria**

HAZARDOUS ECONOMIC GROWTH IN NIGERIA

Nigeria pride herself of owing an economy that is one of Africa's biggest boast. This fact partially explains the country's sustainable political significance in the African continent. She occupies an area of 357,000 square miles (924,000 square kilometers). Nigeria is not particularly large by African standards, but its population of well over a 100 million people makes it the largest demographically, providing a sizable workforce and domestic market. [30]

At independence, agriculture accounted for more than half of all exports and two-thirds of the gross domestic product (GDP). But its importance was soon to decline. Agriculture has now been relegated to a marginal economic role, at least in terms of exports and balance of trade criteria, though not in terms of subsistence farming or employment. The culprit and savior was petroleum. The importance of oil exploration and exports slowly became recognized in the early 1960s. The civil war was partly fought over control of the oil fields and

---

30. Stephen Wright, *Nigeria: Struggle for Stability and Status. Op Cit.* p. 103,

revenues of the southeast, although the intensity of the war slowed the full exploitation of oil fields until the 1970s. [31]

By every socioeconomic and sociopolitical calculations,

> Nigeria had all the makings of an uplifting tale: poor African nation blessed with enormous sudden wealth. Visions of prosperity rose with the same force as the oil that first gushed from the Niger Delta's marshy ground in 1956. The world market craved delta crude, a "sweet," low-sulfur liquid called Bonny Light, easily refined into gasoline and diesel. By the mid-1970s, Nigeria had joined OPEC (Organization of Petroleum Exporting Countries), and the government's budget bulged with petrodollars. Everything looked possible—but everything went wrong.[32]

True to fact, the growth of the oil industry in Nigeria equally paced the ascendancy of a corrupt system of governance in the post civil war Nigeria of the 1970s. And

> the late 1970s witnessed the peak of oil revenues. As a member of the Organization of Petroleum Exporting Countries (OPEC), Nigeria capitalized on the financial gains of the post-1973 period and by the end of the 1970s was touting itself, and respectfully being courted, as the "champion" of Africa. The oil boom also had a crucial impact on the domestic political economy as revenues accrued to the federal government,

---

31. Ibid. p.3
32 *Nigerian Oil, Curse of the Black Gold:Hope and Betrayal in the Niger Delta*, National Geographic Magazine, February 2007

increasing its influence over state governments within the country. These "easy-come" revenues led to a profligate federal government, which sprayed money on projects and policies with little regard for the broader problems involved. Such wealth also accentuated the trend of corruption within the polity, raising it to an art form in the Second Republic. By the mid- 1980s the golden age had already passed, and by the early 1990s Nigeria was facing critical economic and political conditions. Its failure to diversify from a single traded commodity, albeit oil, put the country in a precarious position, as did its failure to develop more substantial trade relations within the African continent. Nigeria's important role in creating the Economic Community of West African States (ECOWAS) in 1975 did not translate into making that a very meaningful organization. [33]

The weak economic foundation that was laid for the young and morally fragile country continues to yield the dividend of corruption and lawlessness even in the present political dispensation. The enormity of the anomalous challenge has made the country into a corrupt octopus.

Within Nigeria there was the initial general agreement about the good will of the then President Olusegun Obasanjo to move Nigeria forward in all dimensions. His letter to the house of Assembly after receiving intelligence information on the destiny of Nigeria from

---

33. Ibid

the United States Department of Intelligence bears eloquent testimony to this purposeful good will. He noted to the house that, despite claims to the contrary,

> ... It is important for us to know that we are being rated low, not because of what is happening to us from outside but because of what we do to, for and by our selves internally, No outside power can map the country's present and future for it except God... Those who indulge in such predictions are prisoners of the past. If our detractors cannot see our far-reaching reforms, our fight against waste and corruption, the new culture of produce and service delivery that is gradually emerging, the political reforms including the ongoing National Political Reform Conference as well as the sacrifices our people are making to ensure economic progress and democratic consolidation as indicators of progress and a radical departure from the past, then they must have dubious or diabolical benchmarks for measuring efforts at ensuring oneness, unity, stability, indivisibility, prosperity, development and growth of our dear country.[34]

We can indeed count our blessings and name them one by one with regard to the growth of the Nigerian economy and this growth

---

[34] *THE PUNCH* Newspaper, Wednesday, May 25, 2005 (Nigerian published daily Newspaper)

has been coupled with increasing increments of salaries and arrears of workers within these past years of his tenure of office. We can affirm that primary school teachers can now afford to own cars without credit cards; but whether they can fuel them in the ensuing circumstances is a different matter all together. Unfortunately, the overriding stories of the embezzlement of funds marked for the infrastructural development of the country by members of the cabinet of the Chief Olusegun Obasanjo administration make the question of the sustainable vision of the president a justice question. A fundamentally unjust system that breeds hunger, homelessness and joblessness, only to satisfy a few can never bring about systemic change. The available evidence of today shows a system that frustrates the common person only to serve the need of a selected few politicians. The economic sacrifices of the common person are constantly being exploited by the rich politicians, leading to a daily drop in the life expectancy of Nigerians. A clearer picture of Nigeria can be gained by looking at the "quick facts" presented by the World Bank Development indicators in April 2005.

Nigeria Quick Facts	2005
Population Total (Millions)	135.6
Population Growth (Annual %)	2.2
Surface area (sq. km) (thousand)	923.8
GNI (Current US $) (Billions)	86.8
GDP per capita, Atlas method (Current US$)	50.2
GDP per capital (constant, 1995) (US $)	275.3
Life expectancy at birth, total (years)	43.8
Mortality rate infant (per 1,000 live at birth	100.0
Prevalence of HIV, total (% of population ages 15-49)	3.9

(Figure 1)[35]

To provide a glimpse of the available econo-statistical data about Nigeria, I refer readers to *Appendix 2* entitled *"Nigeria at a glance"*; together with *Appendix 3 "Nigeria data profile"*; all from the World Bank development indicators. These comparative studies enable us to note with facts and figures the enormity of the myriads of problems that have been bequeathed to the current generations of Nigeria citizenry and which are likely to be passed onto the next

---

[35] World Bank fact sheet 2007

generation if nothing tangible is done to curb the alarming rate of corruption among our greedy rulers. This will be nothing but blatant transmission of economic injustice to the unborn. And injustice anytime, is injustice every time and in every age.

It was with a deep sense of satisfaction that many of us Nigerians studying in the United states and other parts of the world, received the news that our Nigerian Archbishop John Onaiyekan together with Archbishops of other third world countries, (Archbishop Medardo Mazombwe of Lusaka, Archbishop Berhaneyessuys Souraphiel of Ethiopia, Telesphore Cardinal Toppo of India and Oscar Cardinal Rodriguez of Honduras) would meet with Chancellor Gerhard Schroeder (Germany), Prime Minister Tony Blair (Britain), President Jacques Chirac (France) and President Jose Manuel Barroso of the European Commission about debt cancellation in view of the meeting of the G 77 and the consideration of developing country's debt during the World body's meeting.

This is a very welcome development that is a hundred per cent commendable from our Christian faith perspective and also in perfect accord with the challenge of the Holy father Pope Benedict XVI to the Rwandan Bishops on May 21, 2005 during their Ad Limina visits to Rome when he said: "*work* ceaselessly so that the Gospel penetrates ever more deeply into the hearts and lives of believers, inviting the faithful to assume their responsibilities in society, especially in the fields of economy and politics, with a moral sense nourished by the Gospel and the Church's social doctrine."[36]

Even though debt cancellation was eventually granted, and "Nigeria has paid off its multi- billion dollar Paris Club debt, becoming the first African nation to settle with its official lenders,[37]" there is a remaining concern about whether or not Nigerians would have learned any lesson from the experience. The question remain: what is being done today to ensure that the blessing of international debt relief will benefit the people of Nigeria? Have our present leaders stopped looting and storing any available monies in foreign bank accounts? Are we now immune from the greed and money laundering activities of the likes of Alimiasegha , the erstwhile governor of Bayelsa state, who would trade his executive royalty in Britain for Nigeria's wealth loots? President Obasanjo said recently in Paris, France that: *"Funds received from the repatriation of stolen funds from countries like Switzerland as well as funds from debt relief will go directly to sectors such as health, roads, education, water, rural electrification, irrigation and power and these are the sectors that benefit the poor directly."* [38] Yet, in considering the money returned to Nigeria so far from the Sani Abacha's family, one is tempted logically to ask: Where has it gone to? What roads and hospitals or schools benefited from such recovered funds? Similarly,

---

36 Vaticannews.com May 27, 2005
37 Www. British Broadcasting Corporation News (BBC), April 26, 2006
38 Www. AllAfrica.com: Nigeria: Obasanjo: Foreigners encouraged corruption in Nigeria

how is the oil revenue being utilized? President Olusegun Obasanjo was the sole minister for petroleum resources through his tenure of office as the president of the federal republic of Nigeria in eight years. Yet his promises of a better Nigeria were not the least met. The nation is still bedeviled with epileptic power supply. The provision of pipe born water is far from reaching the millennium goal. Schools and Nigerian major highways are in a state of disbelief.

Another reason for fear is the recent plan by the Federal government to retrench about 33,000 workers from the civil service in a country that is already over crowded by unemployment. The hue and cry is not necessarily only about the planned overhaul whether legitimate or its illegitimacy as canvassed by the Congress, but on the economic blunder that is willed behind it. Is it not economically suicidal for a country whose *palm cannel* was broken for her by a benevolent spirit to calculatively attempt to invest in the futility of incurring debt to pay gratuities of planned retrenched workers? Does it not sound bizarre for the "Federal Government to borrow N50 billion from the World Bank to finance the settlement of gratuities of workers to be sacked?"[39] Of what economic benefit will it be to invest in a project that will not accrue economic interest that will self services its debt? According to Adams Oshiomole the president of the Nigerian Labor Congress: ".... Borrowing to retrench is unproductive. The N50 billion loans being contemplated in addition to other cases of

---

[39] www.vanguardngr.com/2002/1118072006.html

piece meal external borrowing is capable of taking the nation back to the dark days of debt overhang. If we must borrow, it must be for productive capital projects, which this retrenchment is not." Only a government vested in corruption will embark on such a mission in futility a*b initio.*

Figure 1 above and Appendices 2 & 3, from the world development indicators show that many Nigerians live on less than a hundred Naira ($1.00) per day, [40] in a country where local government elected officials can afford to buy four brand new cars and where at the same time Senators, federal Ministers and state governors can afford to embank on luxurious journeys abroad that have little or no economic benefit to the country. The indicator also places the life expectancy of an average Nigerian at 45 years. This means that a majority of Nigerians are likely to die young; "after a brief illness" due to untold hardship. Additionally, the research shows that 10 out of a thousand children born in Nigeria are likely to die of curable diseases.

I was shocked during one of my conference trips in October, 2004; when I met some Nigerians in Bangkok Thailand, a country not even as promising as Nigeria in terms of the availability of both human and natural resources, doing menial jobs that ordinarily they would rather not do back home in Nigeria. Moreover, there are

---

[40] This is less than one dollar a day and constitutes living below the certified poverty level according to the statistics of the World Bank.

significant numbers of Nigerians in developed countries such as the United States, Britain, France, Germany, and Italy. And some of our most erudite graduates are taxi drivers and under paid security men and women and Hospital cleaners. I can not count the number of times I have been told at international conferences that Nigeria has no reason to be poor or to beg for debt cancellation when some of her citizens (partisan politicians and erstwhile politicians) are among the richest persons in the world. They actually spend their stolen money from Nigeria to build the economies of those countries where they choose to hide their loot and buy expensive properties and stock shares.

Yet, Nigerians are always on the queue in almost all the known embassies in the world looking for visas to travel in search of greener pastures. A good number of our bright and promising female graduates are on the look out for any available young man with an **"*unknown   international   credentials*"** except   the   title   of **"*Acartarian*"**[41] who can promise to take them across the ocean to a better world. For too often these young women are shocked and humiliated once they arrive at their new homes because the social and economic status of those acclaimed acartarians is not what they have said it was and the promises of life in a new land are not fulfilled. These are signs of failed economic policies retarding the future of the nation and leading to excessive brain drain.

---

[41] This is the local title given to young men / women who are enjoying the privilege of living in any of the developed countries in the world.

A good number of our doctors, nurses, computer experts, and other professionals go overseas only to have their hard earned credentials revalidated on different parameters, while they do extra jobs under their supposed subordinates in learning and professional experience because of the color of their skin and nationality. Will I save words for a number of our highly gifted and intelligent Catholic priests who have studied and lived overseas for ages and who are still treated with reservations because of their origin yet, they dread coming back home because they would suffer in a country riddled with corruption even in sacred places?

Many Nigerians pay so much and engage in all kinds of political and legal wrangling with the goal of becoming citizens of other people's lands. Many among them boast of not returning to Nigeria, the land of injustice, suffering, and confusion. Their children, born to them in a foreign land, may never fully identify themselves as Nigerian and may have no dreams of knowing their kindred or their ancestral land of origin. Why must this be? Is home not home after all? Who are we then? Are Nigerians cursed to be Nigerians? Americans train Americans to love, be proud of America, and to stand shoulder high among other nationals patriotically. What stops Nigerians from entertaining national pride; if not poverty caused by the economic policies of bad government agencies over time?

The point to reflect upon here is the fact that the pain of the "snail paced" economy of Nigeria is only being felt by the poor masses that have no access to the *"political salt sharing"*. It often happens that whenever there is an incremental increase in worker's salaries in Nigeria, the next Presidential broadcast will announce an increase in fuel prices that will affect the overall cost of living, including house rents; as if to maintain the status quo and eliminate the growth of the middle class. Any attempt to plot the graph of Nigeria's economic reform will show that the brunt of the much celebrated economic reform is to a greater extent borne by carrier civil servants and the common people of Nigerian who have no direct access to the wealth of the country like the politicians do.

If our economic reform is going to lead to economic acceleration, then even those at the highest level of governance must share the cost and pains of reform. This should be a collective responsibility rather than being a cost paid by the poor.

There is no doubt that the on-going reforms in the areas of privatization, pension, procurement, and public/private sector partnerships among others are being backed with appropriate laws to ensure the security of investors, but what visible guarantee do we have that politicians are not manipulating variables to maintain the status quo? President Obasanjo rightly opined that: "our political reforms will ensure that there will be no political upheavals both before and after 2007. The on-going political reforms and the outcome of the national political reforms conference are bound to strengthen political structures, eliminate previous political constraints, build new bridges of dialogue and understanding and further consolidate our democratic enterprise"[42]. I dare say without fear of contradiction that these will amount to the traditional Nigerian empty promises of politics if they are not backed up with grassroots mobilization and the civic education of our youths, who are already nurtured in the culture of corruption and maladministration.

2.2 ENDEMIC POVERTY IN NIGERIA

The Cambridge Advance learner's dictionary defined poverty as that state of being extremely poor. If we reflect on the empirical fact that Nigeria has had forty six years of enduring poverty while at the same time possessing many rich resources and rare opportunities for economic prosperities that have been developed during these years of independence, then we can deductively conclude that the presence of endemic poverty in Nigeria shows that something is terribly wrong. Moreover, poverty as an evil does not blossom in isolation. On a macro level, "poverty is a result of corrupt leadership and retrograde cultures that impede modern development."[43]

In analyzing the concept of poverty, it is equally pertinent to highlight causes of poverty. I acknowledge that poverty could be the result of illiteracy, laziness, corruption and other facts. Yet, in this thesis I will focus most fully on how corruption causes and contributes to poverty.

---

[42] Ibid
[43] Jeffrey, D. Sachs. The end of Poverty: Economic Possibilities for our Time (New York, The Penguin Press 2005)p.56

Without making the overgeneralized statement that all Nigerians are hard working I suggest that we consider the excellent work of many Nigerians home and abroad and conclude that Nigeria's poverty is not due to laziness or an unwillingness to work hard. With regard to illiteracy, UNICEF still rates the illiteracy level of Nigeria as rather high. However, considering the number of students who write the Joint Admission and Matriculation Board (JAMB) examinations every year seeking admission into tertiary institutions, coupled with the number of Nigerian graduates produced every year both in Nigeria and overseas, it would be preposterous to contend that Nigerians are academically mediocre and that the limited intelligence of the Nigerian people is a primary factor contributing to their poverty. The recent declaration of President Obasanjo, with regards to his government's reform supported my point when it officially stated:

> Many of those working with my administration are young, creative and patriotic professionals and their job tenures go beyond 2007. They can be relied upon to continue the reform. Also Nigerians, professionals and our society, showing their appreciation for our democratic system and seeing the dividends of reform are beginning to own the policies and programs and are now insisting on transparency, accountability, due process and fair competition.[44]

The truth remains that poverty in Nigeria is caused primarily by the denial of access of the vast majority of Nigerians to the rich

---

[44]www.AllAfrican.com; Op cit

resources of the country by a selected few privileged politician elites. In the preceding pages I have discussed the unquantifiable measure of natural and human wealth with which God has endowed the country. The experience of poverty in Nigeria therefore is caused by an unholy imbalance in the distribution of the abundant national goods and a breakdown in public services that are in turn the result of corrupt practices over time. Moreover, we might began to bring a Christian faith perspective to bear in evaluating poverty and corruption in Nigeria by turning to Joseph Cardinal Ratzinger (now Pope Benedict XVI) and his reflections on the human person in relation to the worlds. Specifically, Ratzinger wrote:

> The teaching about the universal distribution of goods in creation is not merely a beautiful idea; it needs to work in practice. That is why we find associated with it the truth that each individual needs his own sphere of basic necessity of life and that there must be some principle governing the disposal of property, which each and everyone of us must respect. Corresponding to this, of course, raises a pressing need for social legislation to monitor and restrain the misuse of property.[45]

The sad story of our beloved country is that the very makers of the laws are the key breakers of the very laws they legislated. Moreover, by engaging in corrupt practices they violate commonly

---

[45] Ratzinger, Joseph Cardinal, <u>God and the World: a Conversation with Peter Seewald</u> (San Francisco Ignatius Press 2002) p.179.

held human and Christian understandings of the basic rights of human beings.

It is a general belief all over the world that education does not only enhance national productivity and increase the quality of the labor force; it is thought to be one of the best medicines for helping to cure poverty. But present day experiences in Nigeria tend to contradict this rule. Many parents who labored long and hard to send their children to school with the hope that their investment would pay off with the graduation of their children from school are among the most unfortunate people in Nigeria today. They often find themselves still feeding and clothing these same graduates they had painfully invested so much on. Moreover, children who have graduated from college with excellent results and who were thought to be the messiahs of their families are now, many years after graduation, roaming the streets jobless and often frustrated.

The buoyancy of a national economy can be gauged by the level of employment measured against unemployment at a particular point in time in any given country. In a research on the **"Evolution and Welfare of Poverty in Nigeria"** carried out in 1995, it was revealed that the rate of unemployment among those who graduated from college was rising astronomically. For example, whereas the unemployment rate in 1985 was calculated to be 28.6%, in 1986 it rose to 30.1% and then climbed at an alarming rate to 76% in 1987[46]. Today (in 2007), the level of our youths and young adults the unemployment rate is estimated to be 98.9%. This may be a conservative estimate. When we add up the total number of those dismissed by the different tiers of government (in the name of reform), since the inception of the democratic regime in 1999, and the numbers of unemployed university, polytechnic, and college of education graduates with the number of uncompensated secondary and technical school teachers, it may be that close to 99.99% of Nigeria's youth and young adults lacking paid employment.

The aforementioned document also shows how poverty in Nigeria has different faces in the various socio-economic groupings. _"Those with no education comprise the poor and extreme poor, and this is very true in rural areas. It was equally observed that if the head of the household is old, then the probability of their being poor increases. Wage workers and self-employed are often poor. Households with large families with large number of children are frequently poor."[47]_ This pattern of socio-economic structure which shows how easy it is for families to slide into poverty is indicative of the absence of the provision of the necessary social security for the populace by the government; such that the foundations of economic stability for a majority of the people is built on a subjective and

---

[46] Sudharshan, Canagarajah, et al. Nigeria-Poverty Assessment: The Evolution of Poverty and Welfare in Nigeria 1985-1995; (Washington DC, World Bank; July 19, 1995)
[47] ibid

indeterminable factors in life rather than on the indices of the overall national economy. If the educated people are condemned to poverty, what then will happen to the peasant? They will most likely live in dehumanizing misery. The same research further revealed a fundamental error when it discovered that,

> Despite the scope for improving agricultural growth and the poverty focus of existing agricultural programs in-Nigeria- about 87% of the core poor in 1986 and about 89% of the hard core poor in 1992 are engaged in some form of agriculture. The link of depth and severity in poverty 97% and 97.9% respectively in 1986 are agriculture; the same trend shown in 1992.[48]

Many Nigerians are forced everyday to ask the rhetorical questions: What has happened to the balm in Gilead? When will the superficiality of our economic reform end? We have had programs in the past like: *Better life for rural Women, Green Revolution, Mass Mobilization Social and Economic Reform   (MAMSER), and the Structural Adjustment Program (SAP),* organized by the different military regimes and the first ladies of the different military heads of state of the Federal Republic of Nigeria. Such programs often presumed to empower the poor masses, have not had any evident liberative results in Nigerian history.

---

[48] Ibid

Today   *"operation- use- your –opportunity"* is being promoted by the government to encourage people to form NGO-funded pilot projects. However, the reality of the situation is that the Wives of state Governors (First Ladies) of Nigeria have manipulated this initiative and used the names of poor market women to obtain monetary grants from international organizations which they have dubiously used to enrich their already over-fed bank accounts abroad. The poor unlettered market women are often exploitatively gratified with a piece of 'Adire' *(cheap locally woven cotton).*

In his message for the World Day of Peace (1998), Pope John Paul 11 denounced all forms of exploitation like these found in Nigeria as inimical to peace and justice. According to him, those who need particular social and spiritual attention are:

> ... the marginalized, the poor, and victims of all kinds of exploitation.... people who are experiencing in their own flesh the absence of peace and the terrible effects of injustice. Who can remain indifferent to their craving for a life rooted in justice and genuine peace? It is everyone's responsibility to ensure that they achieve their desire; there can be no complete justice unless everyone shares in it equally[49].

The poor are becoming poorer in a downward spiral because of governmental corruption and mismanagement, while the rich are becoming richer by feeding on the exploitation of the poor. This

---

49 John Paul 11, Pope. "World Day of Peace Message" January 1, 1998.

palpable evil of injustice and hunger calls for collective action on behalf of justice for the poor and oppressed. *"We must seek (the solutions) together so that we will no longer have, side by side, the starving and the wealthy, the very poor and the very rich, those who lack the necessary means and others who lavishly waste them. Such contrasts between poverty and wealth are intolerable for humanity."[50]*

After all is said and done, education still remains the most effective way to promote change for us in Nigeria. This must be more than cheap education or mere propaganda. It must be a pedagogical education of the oppressed, an education that will bring about a profound social rebirth and inaugurate a new form of existence for all based upon solidarity with the poor and oppressed. Such an education must meet the challenge issued by Pope John Paul 11 in his address to a General Audience in November 13, 1996,   when he stated that: "every effort must be urgently made to wipe out the scandal of the coexistence of persons who lack the basic essentials with others have a superabundance."[51]

It does appear that the joyful expectation of Nigerian at the dawn of the new democratic era with regards to job security, improved quality of life, etc. is constantly being betrayed by the insensitive economic proposals of the incumbent government. Commenting on the proposed retrenchment of 33,000 workers by the

---

[50] Pope John Paul 11: "Address to World Food Summit," November 13, 1996.
[51] www.vaticannews.com

Federal government as a disservice to the Nigerian populace, the president of the Nigeria Labor Congress opined that:

> "In poverty terms, retrenching 33,000 civil servants will have implications for the survival of additional 231,000 spouses and children as well as about 100,000 extended family dependants. It will also lead to higher mortality, worsen the school dropout ratio, escalate social tension, increase the crime rate and exacerbate such social dysfunctions like prostitution as coping strategies among dependants."[52]

If Nigeria is going to be on a fast track of economic emancipation that will salvage the poverty index of the people, then those charged with the affairs of governance must be taught to realize the dividing line between social economic reform and social euthanasia.

2.3 Corruption and Lawlessness in Nigeria

Corruption thrives most fully within a lawless system in which moral values are downplayed. In such a system, inequality before the law thrives and may even become the norm. Many historians have time without number traced the chaotic social arrangements of most African societies and third world countries to the carefree attitude

---

[52] www.vanguardngr.com/2002/1118072006.html, Tuesday July 18, 2006

with which their erstwhile colonial masters- in the case of Nigeria, the British government- ruled the countries and then handed them over to their loyalists. A bad foundation spoils the whole super structure, says an old adage.

The Major Kaduna Nzeogu led coup of July 1965, advanced the claim that the coup was necessary to curb the increasing level of lawlessness in the nascent independent Nigeria. However this military government and the others that followed it actually consolidated the spiral of lawlessness in Nigeria and increased it to an unprecedented magnitude. They laid aside constitutionally accepted laws and flouted court orders. They put in place draconian decrees as laws that could override any pre-existing law or constitutional provisions in the event of a conflict. Court rulings, especially when it affected the military authority were treated with levity. For example; "the General Yakubu Gowon led military government issued a decree setting aside the Supreme Court judgment in the Lekanmi versus Western State Government case, castigating the Court for daring to rule against the Government, and contending that their revolutionary accession to power on January 15, 1966, affirmed that the military 'always' had the power to abolish the judiciary".[53] This is the height of a despotic mode of governance.

---

[53] Ovienloba, Andrew (Rev), editor. Democracy and Human Rights in Nigeria: Issues and Perspectives (Benin City, Edo, Nigeria, A JDPC Publications 2002) p.83.

If the court has no independent power, then law and order will not be enforced and the evolution of an effective democratic culture of life will be inhibited. Corruption in a society without an effective court system is more likely to thrive even at the highest levels of government, while accountability and transparency are likely to be thrown over board. We need not ask again why the military governments were not accountable to any person or system. The above quotation says it all. It is a case of might being seen as right.

A good many of the politicians functioning in Nigeria today grew up within and benefited from a corrupt system based upon the exploitation of the people by a military government. In such a system the boss can never be questioned or made to account for his/her actions. One must always obey the orders given. People born in Nigeria within the past forty years of Nigerian independence and who are parts of the ruling cabal today have only the experience and influence of authoritarianism, abuse of power and the unaccountability of men and women with social and political power. Many of these people are not educated about civic rights and responsibilities. Since many of them have now moved into positions of social and political leadership we can ask: Where will the wisdom come from for transparent and accountable governance? Most likely, such leaders will strive to maintain corrupt practices and contrive to maintain a system within which a presiding Judge in the court of law cannot rule against the person having the mantle of power for fear of being removed from the seat.

The excessive military incursion into Nigeria civic affairs has led to efforts to foster inefficiency within the Nigerian Police Force so that the police cannot challenge the military. However, those efforts have caused a breakdown of law and order in Nigerian society because the police are now ill equipped, underpaid, and generally have low self and social esteem. This has led some members of the Nigerian Police force to accept bribes at the slightest opportunity and to engage in extra-judicial killings at the slightest provocation; thereby making perversion of justice the order of the day. What could be more embarrassing than for the Inspector General of Police to be indicted for allegations of corruption? It only goes to show the trend running through the entire system. If the one to promote law and order is corrupt then where is the hope for change?

According to John Dewey, if democracy has to be born anew in every generation, then education is its necessary midwife. For Nigeria to experience the beauty of democracy there must be a deliberate liberative action that will only come about through effective education. Solutions cannot be attained in abstract terms. Only a critical and analytical education can bring about a desire for law and order and a demand for governmental accountability. Democracy cannot at anytime thrive in a lawless society. Democracy in America for instance, which has come a long way, is what it is because of the culture of respect for law and order and the effectiveness of the police force. Ideally, in a democracy no one should be able to get away with anything defined as unlawful.

Everyone should be answerable to the laws of the land. Thus, ideally, in Nigeria the military generals and the political godfathers such as the Ibrahim Babangidas, the Ubas, and all politicians have the onerous task of modeling lawful patriotism rather than being a law unto themselves that transcends and trespasses the existing laws of the land with impunity. If the military and political leaders continue to give into corruption they will continue to lend credibility to the lie that a person can thrive while acting in socially irresponsible way.

The pervasiveness of corruption in Nigeria has led some to endorse corruption as a way of life. As long as you can buy your way through embarrassing situations you are regarded by some as a hero. Money speaks. This abysmal lawlessness has even entered high places like the churches and mosques where corrupt leaders are sometimes able to bribe religious leaders and may be baptized and even canonized as illustrious children of the faith. In such instance, we might ask: Where is the prophetic mission of our faiths?

For us to be able to restore law and order to our society we must be able to step back to identify and name corruption for what it is. According to Paulo Freire,

> in order for the oppressed to be able to wage the struggle for their liberation, they must perceive the reality of oppression not as a closed world from which there is no exit, but as a limiting situation which they can transform. This perception is

a necessary condition for liberation. It must become the motivating force for liberating action. Nor does the discovery by the oppressed that they exist in dialectical relationship to the oppressor, as his antithesis- that without them the oppressor could not exist-in itself constitute liberation. The oppressed can overcome the contradiction in which they are caught only when this perception enlists them in the struggle to free them.[54]

When Nigeria returned to a democratic system of governance in May, 1999 after years of military dictatorship, the new government was greeted with a lot of blissful euphoria. But little did the people know that the price of a diluted democracy in the guise of freedom was going to be an unabated spiral of violence resulting in a great loss of lives and properties worth millions of Naira within the first few years of this experience of democracy.

Ethnic and religious violence have undermined all measures of law and order in Nigeria today. Uncontrolled lawlessness encouraged by the silence of the federal government coupled with a lack of will power to bring culprits of religious violence in the northern part of the country to justice have definitely made it almost impossible for southerners and Christians to think of the northern part of Nigeria in terms of the national motto of "one Nation, One Destiny, one

---

[54] Freire, Paulo. Pedagogy of the Oppressed (New York, London; The Continuum International Publishing Group Inc, 2000) p.49.

Nigeria". Moreover, can we estimate the millions of Naira being lost to lawless crude oil bunkers in the Niger Delta states of Nigeria?[55] Or is it possible for us to calculate how many lives have been lost to ethnic wars traceable to the handiwork of jobless youths in the Niger Delta? Can we even talk anymore less about cult violence in schools in which all government efforts to diminish the influence of cults has failed? How many students die every year due to the lawless wars of cultic groups in our schools while our law enforcement agents prove to be powerless in their efforts to stop the violence?

What has been done to retired military generals and politicians who import ammunitions for their ethnic militias and who use these militias to secure their own personal wealth through violence? What can we say about the youths who are willing to be instruments of violence and whose lives are often plagued by hunger and idleness? The promise of rewards for those who carry out the violent wishes of corrupt leaders often leads jobless youths to be at the beck and call of the over-fed political lords who are the beneficiaries of the war.

We must at this time of our history engage in a critical education that will enable us to deconstruct and reconstruct our national political and ideological outlook, especially for our youths while not underemphasizing the education of our adults. The foundational resources that I consider invaluable for this purgation of

---

[55] These are some of the rich political leaders in Nigeria who illegally extract and export crude oil for their own personal profit, but nevertheless under the cover of the unwritten protection of the government.

our sick society are to be founded in Catholic theological principles of justice. Generally, modern Catholic social teaching has been described as the best kept secret of the Church because it is not known and embraced by many in the Church. Still, the principles of justice found within modern Catholic social teaching, while grounded in Christian faith traditions, can have a universal appeal and can become the heart of an approach to resist evil in any of its guises.

Overall, as I move towards a discussion of the Catholic theological principles of justice I align myself with Michael J. Himes and Kenneth R. Himes, O.F.M. when they assert:

> In employing Catholic social thought we are aware that the tradition is composed of basic insights and assumptions about human nature, not blueprints for creating the good society. We do not presume that our proposals can claim to be the catholic position on social action and policy. Ours is but an attempt to prod our collective societal imagination by suggesting some ideas about public life that are derived from a communitarian rather than liberal perspective."[56]

---

[56] Himes, Michael J. and Kenneth R. Himes. Fullness of Faith: the Public Significance of Theology (New York Paulist Press 1993) p. 47.

Chapter Three

Catholic Theological Principles of Justice

"The first of the great challenges facing humanity today is that of the truth itself of who is man. The boundary and relation between nature, technology and morality are issues that decisively summon personal and collective responsibility with regard to the attitudes to adopt concerning what human beings are, what they are able to accomplish and what they should be. 'The theological dimension is needed therefore, both for interpreting and for solving present day problems in human society' (Contesimus Annus, 55)."

- Compendium of the Social Doctrine of the Church, 2005; Pp. 6&9

3.0 Introduction

Underlying all Catholic theological reflections is a belief in the inalienable dignity of the human person. The human person is envisioned within the church's social theological discourse as the summit of God's creation and therefore the beneficiary of all God's gifts of nature. Moreover, as Edward DeBerri and James E Hug note, *"For Catholic social thought, the sacred character of human dignity clearly demands that authentic human development not be understood simply as economic development. Full and authentic human development embraces the social, cultural,*

political and spiritual dimensions of human life as well. It involves
developing one's skill and gifts for service to the common good.[57]
Service to the common good is another way of expressing the concept
of good neighborliness which fundamentally requires that society or
the state establish structures of justice which support and liberate all
peoples.[58] The sense of liberation that is espoused here is rooted in the
New Testament ethic of love of God and love of neighbor.

Within Catholic social thought justice is often envisioned as
having an eschatological dimension. That is, from the perspective of
Catholic social thought; all persons come from one source, God, are
saved by the paschal mystery of Jesus Christ, and will return to that
source in the fullness of time. The point of emphasis therefore in the
Catholic theological principles of justice is the fact that the vision of a
common source and common destiny necessarily call for mutuality in
the shaping of the human community for the common good. Social
structures are unjust when members of a community are denied the
right to participate in society and to contribute to or benefit from the
common good of society.   In his World day of peace message of
1999 (article 6), Pope John Paul 11 articulated this communitarian
understanding of society when he said;

> all citizens have right to participate in the life of their
> community: this is a Conviction which is generally shared

---

57 DeBerri, Edward P., et al. Catholic Social Teaching: Our Best Kept Secret
4th Edition (Mary knoll, New York, Orbis Books; 2004)p.20
58 Ibid p.21

today. But this right means nothing when the democratic process breaks down because of corruption and favoritism, which not only obstruct legitimate sharing in the exercise of power but also prevent people from benefiting from community assets and service, to which everyone has a right.

The problem of corruption in Nigeria society can be explored in the light of Catholic theological principles of justice through a consideration of the following:

- ➢ **The dignity and equality of the human person**
- ➢ **The principle of solidarity**
- ➢ **The principle of subsidiarity**
- ➢ **The principle of common good**
- ➢ **The principle of a preferential option for the poor**

3.1 The Dignity and Equality of the Human Person

This principle is anchored in the strong belief of the Church that all of humanity has been created in the image and likeness of God and that each person possesses a basic dignity and equality that does not come from the laws of the society but that is intrinsic to his/her nature as a human being. In other words, this identity or dignity "cannot be reduced or denied in the name of some collective good. It is to maintain that the goal of society is to develop and enrich the individual human person."[59]

The principle of human dignity recognizes the social nature of the human person and the person as endowed with rights and responsibilities. The rights are numerous and include those basic or essential things that make life truly human. Corresponding to these rights are obligations or duties and responsibilities that entail respect for the rights of others and a call to work for the common good of all. According to the *Catechism of the Catholic Church (CCC)*, "respect for human dignity demands that people not become too attached to goods (temperance), honor each other's rights and needs (justice) and be in solidarity with all."[60] According to this principle, then, *corruption, which is the bane of Nigerian society, can be defined as an excessive attachment to goods (intemperance), an unjust denial of the right of some people's access to a common pool of social goods which becomes unjust and a refusal to be in solidarity with all in obedience to an individual's identity as a human person.*

3.2 The principle of solidarity

One of the gains of the present day democracy in Nigeria for which many Nigerians fought and died is a sense of freedom and self

---

[59] Himes, Michael J. et al. Fullness of Faith: the Public Significance of Theology, Op Cit. p.38.
[60] DeBerri, Edward et al. op cit p.115; The Catechism of the Catholic Church n. 2407

determination. However, soon after we gained this freedom new challenges for which were not prepared, surfaced. Foremost among these new challenges was the drift towards individualism. This individualistic mentality has led or contributed to religious intolerance, exploitation of one's kindred, ritual killings of parents, children and siblings seeking the acquisition of quick wealth and a destructive sense of self interest at the expense of others irrespective of whoever they may be.

Individualism as the very word suggests, involves a turning away from the communitarian spirit of the traditional African society. The word "communitarianism" is somewhat synonymous with the word "solidarity". In discussing solidarity the Church stresses the unity and oneness of the human family. The theological insight grounding the concept of solidarity is that we are all part of the human family irrespective of our race or ethnicity, religion, family, and economic or ideological groupings. All of us as human beings belong to one God as our source and are answerable to God as our ultimate destiny. Our differences, then, are accidental. Moreover, our differences may enrich our lives and be a cause for celebration. Overall, the principle of solidarity affirms that "a healthy society is characterized by a variety of intermediate groups freely flourishing between the individual and the state. Within society there needs to be a plethora of organizations which allows for social interaction and promote the individual's participation in group activity."[61]

---

[61] Himes, Michael J., et al. Fullness of Faith, Op cit., p.38.

The focus here is clearly on the spirit of social connectedness, and participation in the social activities of the state. The human person is by nature social and realizes him/herself within a socially interactive context. The *Catechism of the Catholic Church* article 1879 says: *"The human person needs to live in society. Society is not for him an extraneous addition but a requirement of his nature. Through the exchange with others, mutual service and dialogue with his brethren, man develops his potential; he thus responds to his Vocation."*

In his encyclical **Sollicitudo Rei Socialis** (On Social Concern, n.39), Pope John Paul 11 defines solidarity as a social mutuality. The document states that,

> the exercise of solidarity within each society is valid when its members recognize one another as persons. Those who are more influential because they have a greater share of goods, and common services, should feel responsible for the weaker and be ready to share with them all they possess. Those who are weaker, for their part, in the same spirit of solidarity, should not adopt a purely passive attitude or one that is destructive of the social fabric, but, while claiming their legitimate rights, should do what they can for the good of all. The intermediate groups, in their turn, should not selfishly insist on their particular interest, but respect the interest of others.

The principle of solidarity detests every form of opportunistic exploitation of the weak either economically or politically. With this in mind then, **corruption can be defined as any act of greed or anti social behavior that denies a fellow human being equal opportunity in the share of societal goods for the purpose of individual selfish interest.** Corruption by this understanding becomes a social sin that cries to heaven for restoration because it wounds the natural bond of love that should exist within the social circle of humans.

3.3 The Principle of Subsidiarity

One of the building blocks of democracy is a sense of popular participation. Popular participation here does not by any means diminish the importance of social structure in society. Instead there is a call for popular participation within democracies so that all may have the opportunity to contribute to the structuring or realization of the common good of society.

Even though the Catholic Church is not a democracy, but a divinely inspired hierarchical structure, it extols those principles and qualities that strongly uphold the dignity and worth of individual persons within a given social interaction. The operational principle within the Church that focuses on mutual social roles and responsibilities is called subsidiarity.

The principle of subsidiarity states that, *"a community of a higher order should not interfere in the internal life of a community of a lower order, depriving the latter of its functions, but rather should support it in case of need and help to co-ordinate its activity with the activities of the rest of society, always with a view to the common good."[62]* The principle of subsidiarity is opposed to the over-centralization of power and collectivism. An identification of corrupt practices in Nigeria, therefore, using the principle of subsidiarity will focus on the over- centralization of resource control and the police force, presidential interference with state and local politics and executive dominance of the legislative and judicial arms of government.

It is important to note here that the principle of subsidiarity does not in any way endorse an absolutizing of the power of subordinate bodies; rather, it highlights the importance of respect for individual initiatives within a legal framework of roles and responsibilities. The principle of subsidiarity calls us to combine respect for the dignity and worth of the human person with a concern for structures of solidarity that contributes to the common good of the society as a whole. While subsidiarity can bring about orderliness, cohesiveness and organizational strength to a society, its abuse could diminish or destroy the free flow of goods and service delivery.

Corruption from the foregoing analysis, can pass here for: **a violation of thc fundamental human rights of a people when they are denied because of governmental fraud and oppressive**

---

[62] The *Catechism of the Catholic Church* (Paulist Press, CD ROM Edition)nos. 184

manipulations, the right to choose how and who should govern them through a free and fair election, popular participation in decision making, and the right for transparent and accountable leadership. Corruption may also negatively affect the delegation of power to the different levels of government as required by due process in democratic states. Generally, *"The principles of subsidiarity and pluralism in Catholic social theory reflect the tradition's appreciation for natural communities like families, neighborhoods, and ethnic groups. "*[63]

As the principle of subsidiarity challenges government to involve all in governance, it emphasizes that:

> It is important for government to have oversight and review in a structured manner so as to avoid local corruption and test performance, but processes to establish accountability should flow both ways.... Reconfiguring public services along lines that utilize community-based organizations is a venture that might enable individuals to have greater voice in the design and assessment of public service agencies.[64]

3.4 The Principle of the Common Good

Gadium ET Spes, the pastoral constitution on the Church that was developed by the Fathers of the Second Vatican Council, define the

---

[63] Himes Michael J. et al op cit p.47
[64] Ibid p.49

common good as *"the sum total of the social conditions which allow people, either as groups or as individuals, to reach their fulfillment more fully and more easily."*[65] In order for us to have an opportunity to grow and develop fully and realize our human potential, a certain measure of social fabric must exist within our societies. This necessary social provision is what is referred to as the common good. The common good concerns the life of all in the society without any form of discrimination. It calls for prudence from each, and even more from those who exercise social and political authority.

The principle of the common good calls on all to realize the "inherent integrity to all of creation which requires careful stewardship of all of our resources, ensuring that we use and distribute them justly and equitably as well as planning for future generations."[66] More fully, the principle of common good consists of three essential elements.

First, the common good presupposes respect for the human person as such. In the name of the common good, public authorities are bound to respect uphold and defend the fundamental human rights of all. Chief among these rights are rights to freedom of conscience, privacy, and rightful freedom as in matters of religion.

Secondly, the tenet of the common good demands that the government provides the enabling structures necessary for the

---

[65] The Documents of the Vatican 11: *Gadium Et Spes* n.26
[66] Www.Catholic Relief Services (CRS).

attainment of social well being and development of the group itself. In other words *"it should make accessible to each what is needed to lead a truly human life: food, clothing, health, work, education and culture, suitable information, the right to establish a family. ... "[67]*

Thirdly, the common good requires peace, that is, the stability and security of a just order. It presupposes that authority should ensure by morally acceptable means the security of society and its members. It is the basis of the right to legitimate personal and collective defense.[68]

Corruption then is **the deprivation to the members of a community, nay Nigeria, of the basic needs of life through culpable acts of misappropriation of funds, bad administrative prioritization, and the absence of achievable good will on the part of the government toward the governed.** The salient point to be assimilated here is that when a social theory emphasizes the promotion of the common good as much as the regulation of self-interest, a more positive view of the socio-political structure becomes an attainable possibility.

---

[67] Sirico, Robert A. (Rev.) et al. The Social Agenda of the Catholic Church (London/New York, Burns and Oates, 2000 Pontifical Council for Justice and Peace)p.83.
[68] Ibid; see also; *CCC* nn. 1906-1909

3.5 The Principle of a Preferential Option for the Poor

At the heart of the gospel message of Jesus Christ is a care and concern for the poor. In the beatitudes of the Sermon on the Mount, Jesus declared the poor blessed because the kingdom of God belongs to them.[69]

The preferential option for the poor holds that the way society responds to the needs of the poor through its public policies is the litmus test of its justice or injustice.[70] The principle states that *"the deprivation and powerlessness of the poor wounds the whole community. The extent of their suffering is a measure of how far we are from being a true community of persons. These wounds will be healed only by greater solidarity with the poor and among the poor themselves."[71]*

From the perspective of this principle, poverty and suffering, even though they have eschatological value, are far removed from the original plan of God. This is even more so in the case of poverty resulting from injustice and maladministration. It behooves the rich and powerful therefore to see it as their social responsibility to care for the poor and vulnerable if they are going to be just.

According to this option for the poor, workers, the aged, the disabled and the mentally retarded, which are often exploited and

---

[69] Matt 5:3; Luke 6:20
[70] United States Bishops, *Economic Justice for All*, n.123
[71] Ibid n.88

unduly taken advantaged of, have a right to respect and support. Governmental policies, therefore, that do not take into consideration the plight of the poor and vulnerable in the society are evil and do not merit the obedience of all.

As seen in the light of an option for the poor, **corruption can be judged to be the political and economic exploitation of the economically poor, the mentally/physically challenged and politically disadvantaged persons in the society because of their unprovided helplessness.** Genuine action on behalf of the poor must include efforts to determine why the poor are poor and a striving to foster economic and spiritual liberation from poverty. Moreover, a program that serves to maintain the poor in their poverty rather than liberating them becomes a social sin that wounds not only the poor but the entire human race.

Now, having analytically discussed the origin/ dynamics of corruption in Nigeria in the light of an understanding of Catholic theological principles of justice at some length; let us now proceed to examine the possibility of curing Nigeria of the evils of corruption.

Chapter Four

Solving the Nigerian Endemic Corruption Equation

The immediate purpose of the Church's social doctrine is to propose the principles and values that can sustain a society worthy of the human person.
- Compendium of the Social Doctrine of the Church, 2005; p.253.

4.0 Introduction

C hange is a phenomenon that is often too difficult to assimilate. Yet, without change, society can not progress. In talking about change special emphasis must be placed on constructive change that is informed by good will and directed towards the common good.

To address the problem of corruption in Nigeria, it is of utmost relevance to note that because of the degree and dynamics of corruption a multi-dimensional approach is needed. In the first place, there is a need for reasonable political good will from the government. Secondly there must be a grassroots approach to promoting generational transformation of the entire social fabric of the Nigerian polity. That is, everybody must come to recognize the reality of the evil of corruption and the need to eradicate it from the social system both for the good of the present and future generations. Now, in developing an approach for addressing corruption the Catholic theological principles of justice become relevant on both horizontal and vertical levels.

4.1 Facing the Challenges of Transformation in Nigeria

On the vertical level, which has to do with what currently exists in Nigerian society, there must be a deliberate shift in ideology. The lucrative game of corruption must become unnecessary and unattractive. On the one hand, both the state and federal government must make provisions (social security) to care for pensioners, the unemployed, and others within the category of the less privileged. When basic human needs, especially economic and medical security, are not guaranteed, then the temptation to turn to corruption to gather for the future can become great. As Dike observed, "…. becoming corrupt is almost unavoidable (in Nigeria), because morality is relaxed in the society, and many people struggle for survival without assistance from the state." (Dike, June, 2003). On the other hand, those caught in the act of corruption within the circles of governance must be seen by all to be duly prosecuted according to the laws of the land. The application of selective justice that exonerates the big politicians from being made to face the wrath of the law must be made and seen to change.

When the ancient Greek philosopher Plato said that those who aspire to be rulers must be trained as philosophers, his idea of a philosopher king was not far removed from the views of those who know the dynamics of leadership. In his political philosophy, Plato reasoned thus, that:

> The political structure of the just city [should] depend on a thorough educational program, which selects the potential philosophers on the basis of merit, without regard to class or gender, and trains them ultimately to know and love the forms, through which each person progresses to his or her maximal level of ability. Such an education must begin by training the appetites and spirit to accede to the rule of reason…Once the philosophers are selected their autocratic rule in the light of reason must be safeguarded from corruption. Therefore, they are to be deprived of private property and families, and forced to pay attention to civic affairs instead of only contemplating the forms. Such drastic measures alone can ensure that their

rule is for the sake of the city as a whole and not for their private interests.[72]

If we reason with the spirit of the ancient Philosopher in the choice of people with which to entrust the power of leadership of society, we will understand better why the idea that anybody, irrespective of a past record of corruption can ascend to a leadership role without a sound background check must be reversed. Anyone seeking a political appointment must express an understanding of leadership that is in consonance with the principles of solidarity, - i.e., a commitment to service for all, and not just for a clandestine political party or family agenda-, subsidiarity, which is the willingness to share power so that there is transparency and accountability in governance as stipulated by the laws, and an option for the poor- i.e., equal opportunity for all- for the ultimate purpose of the common good. The idea of absolute secrecy in governance must also be eliminated as this breeds corruption to a very great degree. In the words of Maathai Waarati, *"Secret transactions between foreign stakeholders and the minister of finance should end. The responsibility to end corruption in such deals should be a responsibility of those who borrow as well as those who lend. The lenders cannot pretend that they do not care what the*

---

[72] Microsoft® Encarta® Reference Library 2002. © 1993-2001 Microsoft

Corporation. All rights reserved: Plato's "Political theory and Ethics" *borrower does with the borrowed funds. Not when those who have to re-pay the loans are hostage to a dictatorial system or are unaware of the secret deals. No bank would operate like that in any neighborhood. Why should it be different in the World Bank and in world capitals?"[73]*

Second, the endemic problem of corruption in Nigeria must be addressed on the horizontal level that is, the level of looking from the present to the horizon of the future and considering possibilities for social transformation. On this level the Church and other social interest groups can play an active role. It is here that civic education and empowerment of the masses is also needed.

More fully, drawing from the wisdom of Christian traditions, the Churches must take an active role by teaching principles of justice. In this regard, the Churches in Nigeria can borrow from the United States' bishops, who stated that,

> Our social doctrine must also be an essential part of the curriculum and life of our schools, religious education programs, sacramental preparation, and Christian initiation activities. We need to share and celebrate our common social heritage as Catholics, developing materials and training tools

---

[73] Waarati, Maathai. Op Cit.

that ensure that we are sharing our social teaching in every educational ministry of our parishes[74]

In order to foster positive social transformation, the liturgical provisions in the Roman Missale for praying for Justice and Peace, the Oppressor, and Public leaders[75] should not be treated as secondary any longer. Instead, they should be emphasized. Overall, the Church must develop an intentionally prophetic outreach. The social concern of the Christian churches must not end with the issuing of communiqué at the end of each Episcopal conference; Communiqué which, by the way, are often now treated as unimportant and that are never implemented. Rather, a curriculum of catechesis that incorporates the doctrines of Catholic Social Teaching, with emphasis on the principles of justice, must be developed. Additionally, pastors of churches must see such catechesis as important and as such meriting their particular attention. Such catechesis must be presented by pastors and trained Catechists rather than by unskilled Catechists.

The Basic Christian Communities (BCCs) should be used to teach principles of justice against corruption among the Christian communities in Nigeria. Every diocese and parishes in Nigeria must be made to present a curriculum for social justice with equal

---

[74] United States Catholic Bishops Conference, *"Communities of Salt and Light,"* 1993; see also www.osjspm.org

[75] The Roman Missile, (The Sacramento). (New York, Catholic Book Publishing Co. 1985) nn. 17-22, 30,42 &45

emphasis. There is also a need to develop a system that helps to check the progress of the program. In obedience to the principle of subsidiarity, a diocesan synod could also be held where the services of experts in the field are employed to develop specific ways of teaching about principles of Catholic social teaching and other related issues on both macro/micro levels. I dare say if the Church alone implements a consistent program of this nature in a timely manner the enormity of the problem will be minimized.

Another opportunity for an effective program of social change can be found within the secular order or the civil society. What has to be done and who is to do it here must be clearly defined. The principles of justice, even though they are tools developed within the Catholic Church, have a universal relevance and can serve as a resource in the broader society as a whole.

In *"Economic Justice for All"* the United States Bishops declared: *"Where the effects of past discrimination persist, society has an obligation to take positive steps to overcome the legacy of injustice. Judiciously administered affirmative action programs in education and employment can be important expressions of the drive for solidarity and participation that is at the heart of true justice. Social harm calls for social relief."*[76]   In drawing from the example provided by the United States' bishops, the Nigerian

---

[76] "Economic Justice for All" Pastoral Letter on Catholic Social Teaching and the US Economy By the United States Catholic Bishops, 1986

Catholic hierarchy must endeavor to take positive steps in galvanizing other religious bodies for sustainable systemic change in Nigeria. This is where ecumenical bodies like the Christian Association of Nigeria (CAN) can become very relevant. The benefits of past inter-religious dialogues could also be taken advantage of to galvanize our Muslim brethren to become partners for change since a large number of Nigerians are Muslims and they will also benefit from an anti-corruption campaign. More so, given the universal nature of the problem of corruption and the anticipated benefit the program portends for all Nigerians, the interest of all relevant bodies must be elicited. Thus, the next major religious body to be incorporated in this all important project is the umbrella body of the Islamic conference of Nigeria to mobilize the Muslim communities. Moreover, the roles of the non governmental organizations (NGOs) should not be underrated. However, from the benefit of my experience, I contend that care must be taken not to elicit the services of those NGOs that are benefiting from the evils of the system of corruption as they will only serve to sabotage this effort.

In working out this massive anti-corruption campaign, the Catholic Secretariat of Nigeria (CSN), under the auspices of the directorate of Church and Society- Justice Development and Peace Committee (JDPC), could serve as the primary agent for facilitating the campaign. The JDPC helped to monitor the 2003 general elections in Nigeria successfully, and continues to exist as a very effective national coalition. This coalition could be further mobilized for a national anti-corruption campaign.

4.2 A Practical Proposal for a Decisive Action against Corruption in Nigeria

If the problem of corruption is going to be addressed on a long term basis for a long term effect, then the need for civic education as a compulsory subject at all levels of education in Nigeria is inevitable. Passing a course on civic education that has anti-corruption principles of justice must be made as compulsory as passing English language and mathematics exams to enter into any higher institutions of learning in Nigeria. Along the same lines, groups such as peace clubs in schools should be encouraged to flourish in all secondary schools with the backing of the Ministry of Education under the close monitoring of a body such as a "National *Peace Educators Network*" (or whatever name we choose to call it) backed by law.

A curriculum could be developed for the effective teaching of Catholic Social Doctrine in all Catholic schools. I will suggest we begin with a few demonstration Schools on a micro-level as a pilot project for one year. During this pilot program, a collaborative network could be formed with other organized bodies across the world with same vision of peace and justice education. The importance of projects like this was clearly articulated by the US

Bishops in 1993 in a document entitled *"Communities of Salt and Light"*. The U.S. Bishops wrote:

> Our social doctrine must also be an essential part of the curriculum and life of our schools, religious education programs, sacramental preparation, and Christian initiation activities. We need to share and celebrate our common social heritage as [a people], developing materials and training tools that ensure that we are sharing our social teaching in every educational ministry of our parishes

Knowledge, we are told, is power. Knowledge for the people spells power to the people; and when the people are empowered in knowledge, they learn to demand a transparent and accountable leadership. This is why we must empower the Nigerian citizenry through civic education using the tools of the Catholic principles of justice, so that they can demand accountable and transparent governance from their governments and local authorities. To do this effectively they need to overcome a lot of ignorance and fear and not yield to violence, for *"while violence can change events, even radically, it does not give power to the people."*[77] Besides, *"violence or armed revolution generally generates new injustices, introduces new imbalances, and causes new disasters; one cannot combat a real*

---

[77] Arbuckle Gerald A. Violence, Society, and the Church (Collegeville, Minnesota, Liturgical Press, 2004)p.234.

evil at the price of a greater evil."[78] Only systematic education can deconstruct and then reconstruct the outlook on the life of a human person in a positive and progressive way.

Every oppressive/corrupt despot knows that it is much easier to govern and exploit people who are poor, ignorant and fearful. Therefore, bad leaders discourage civic education. As seen from the perspective of a psychology of dominance, *"the violator always wants the violated precisely to agree that they are powerless, insignificant, and less than human."*[79] That is why we must not give in to intimidation and discouragement. Education for justice as suggested in this work is an important tool for social change that can pay off in the long run.

It is good to note that in all the different programs of our past and present governments, no one has ever thought about developing educational or curriculum tools that specifically address the problem of corruption for our youths, who are the leaders of tomorrow -even though we do know that the political elites want their children to succeed them in corruption as a closed unquestioned social circle. It has been sufficiently speculated that our current social-political elites do not desire a real change for the better. However, I have argued that Nigeria must be cleansed of corruption and poverty by a renewed

---

[78] Ibid p.235.
[79] Ibid p.232.

commitment to the common good and a concern for the development of all the people of the country.

If this is going to happen, it will take our determined collective "yes" and work to liberate our present and future generations from the evils of corruption. Moreover, we must begin now, without further procrastination, with every citizen joining in the effort so that we can put an end to the sufferings and social malformation that plagues our country.

Appendix 1

Note:

The thickness of the color coupled with the drop in percentage in a descending order, represents the prevalence of corruption in a particular region or country.

Nigeria at a glance

9/20/04

POVERTY and SOCIAL

	Nigeria	Sub-Saharan Africa	Low-income
2003			
Population, mid-year *(millions)*	135.7	703	2,310
GNI per capita *(Atlas method, US$)*	320	480	450
GNI *(Atlas method, US$ billions)*	43.7	347	1,038
Average annual growth, 1997-03			
Population (%)	2.4	2.3	1.9
Labor force (%)	2.6	2.4	2.3
Most recent estimate (latest year available, 1997-03)			
Poverty (% of population below national poverty line)	..	..	..
Urban population (% of total population)	47	36	30
Life expectancy at birth *(years)*	47	46	58
Infant mortality *(per 1,000 live births)*	87	103	82
Child malnutrition (% of children under 5)	..	..	44
Access to an improved water source (% of population)	57	58	75
Illiteracy (% of population age 15+)	32	35	39
Gross primary enrollment (% of school-age population)	..	87	92
Male	..	94	99
Female	..	80	85

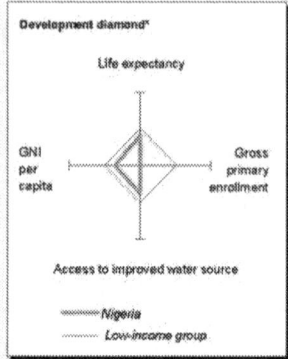

Development diamond*

Life expectancy

GNI per capita — Gross primary enrollment

Access to improved water source

——— Nigeria
- - - - Low-income group

KEY ECONOMIC RATIOS and LONG-TERM TRENDS

	1983	1993	2002	2003
GDP *(US$ billions)*	34.9	21.4	46.7	58.4
Gross domestic investment/GDP	..	23.3	26.1	22.7
Exports of goods and services/GDP	13.6	47.1	40.8	50.0
Gross domestic savings/GDP	10.8	20.2	25.9	31.8
Gross national savings/GDP	8.4	13.2	15.1	20.2
Current account balance/GDP	-14.3	-10.1	-10.9	-2.7
Interest payments/GDP	2.8	4.0	3.3	2.8
Total debt/GDP	50.3	143.8	65.2	60.1
Total debt service/exports	23.6	14.8	15.4	10.4
Present value of debt/GDP	..	..	..	..
Present value of debt/exports	..	..	..	..

	1983-93	1993-03	2002	2003	2003-07
(average annual growth)					
GDP	4.9	2.9	1.5	10.7	5.0
GDP per capita	1.9	0.3	-0.7	8.4	2.7
Exports of goods and services	4.4	2.1	-11.1	32.4	4.5

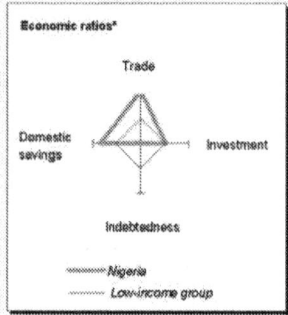

Economic ratios*

Trade

Domestic savings — Investment

Indebtedness

——— Nigeria
- - - - Low-income group

STRUCTURE of the ECONOMY

	1983	1993	2002	2003
(% of GDP)				
Agriculture	33.2	24.2	31.2	26.4
Industry	29.7	58.7	43.8	49.5
Manufacturing	9.9	4.0	4.6	4.0
Services	37.0	17.2	25.0	24.2
Private consumption	71.4	62.3	48.4	44.9
General government consumption	17.7	17.5	24.7	23.3
Imports of goods and services	17.5	50.2	-41.0	40.9

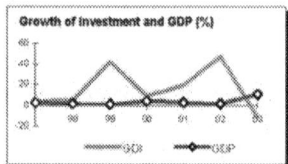

	1983-93	1993-03	2002	2003
(average annual growth)				
Agriculture	4.8	4.0	4.2	4.1
Industry	3.6	1.5	-8.0	22.4
Manufacturing	4.7	2.7	13.7	6.2
Services	6.9	3.3	6.6	9.4
Private consumption	-1.7	-4.4	52.0	-17.1
General government consumption	2.2	13.2	-13.5	10.2
Gross domestic investment	8.5	9.5	47.0	-11.5
Imports of goods and services	-5.8	8.0	11.9	10.8

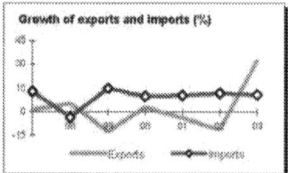

Growth of investment and GDP (%)

Growth of exports and imports (%)

Note: 2003 data are preliminary estimates.

* The diamonds show four key indicators in the country (in bold) compared with its income-group average. If data are missing, the diamond will be incomplete.

Appendix 2 (www.WorldBank.org)

Appendix 3 (www.worldbank.org/nigeriadataprofile)

	2000	2005	2006
People			
Population, total	117.6 million	131.5 million	..
Population growth (annual %)	2.4	2.2	..
Poverty headcount ratio at national poverty line (% of population)	..	..	..
Life expectancy at birth, total (years)	43.8	43.8	..
Fertility rate, total (births per woman)	5.9	5.5	..
Mortality rate, infant (per 1,000 live births)	107.0	100.0	..
Mortality rate, under-5 (per 1,000)	207.0	194.0	..
Births attended by skilled health staff (% of total)	..	..	..
Malnutrition prevalence, weight for age (% of children under 5)	..	..	..

Immunization, measles (% of children ages 12-23 months)	35.0	35.0	..
Prevalence of HIV, total (% of population ages 15-49)	..	3.9	..
Primary completion rate, total (% of relevant age group)	..	81.8	..
School enrollment, primary (% gross)	95.5	102.9	..
School enrollment, secondary (% gross)	..	34.2	..
School enrollment, tertiary (% gross)	..	..	..
Ratio of girls to boys in primary and secondary education (%)	..	..	..
Literacy rate, adult total (% of people ages 15 and above)	..	..	..
Environment			
Surface area (sq. km)	923.8 thousand	923.8 thousand	..
Forest area (sq. km)	131.4 thousand	110.9 thousand	..
Agricultural land (% of land area)	76.9	..	..
CO_2 emissions (metric tons per capita)	0.4	..	..

Improved water source (% of population with access)	..	..	..
Improved sanitation facilities, urban (% of urban population with access)	..	..	..
Energy use (kg of oil equivalent per capita)	759.1	..	..
Energy imports, net (% of energy use)	-125.3	..	..
Electric power consumption (kWh per capita)	77.5	..	..
Economy			
GNI, Atlas method (current US$)	33.5 billion	74.0 billion	..
GNI per capita, Atlas method (current US$)	280.0	560.0	..
GDP (current US$)	46.0 billion	99.0 billion	..
GDP growth (annual %)	5.4	6.9	..
Inflation, GDP deflator (annual %)	38.2	26.9	..
Agriculture, value added (% of GDP)	26.3	23.3	..
Industry, value added (% of GDP)	52.7	56.8	..
Services, etc., value added (% of GDP)	21.0	19.9	..
Exports of goods and services (% of	54.3	53.1	..

GDP)			
Imports of goods and services (% of GDP)	32.2	35.2	..
Gross capital formation (% of GDP)	20.3	20.9	..
States and markets			
Time required to start a business (days)	..	43.0	43.0
Market capitalization of listed companies (% of GDP)	9.2	19.6	..
Military expenditure (% of GDP)	0.8	0.9	..
Fixed line and mobile phone subscribers (per 1,000 people)	5.0	150.6	..
Internet users (per 1,000 people)	0.7	38.0	..
Roads, paved (% of total roads)	..	..	..
High-technology exports (% of manufactured exports)	0.4	..	..
Global links			
Merchandise trade (% of GDP)	64.6	60.2	..
Net barter terms of trade (2000 = 100)	100.0	..	..
Foreign direct investment, net inflows (BoP, current US$)	1.1 billion	2.0 billion	..
Long-term debt (DOD, current	30.2 billion	20.3 billion	..

US$)			
Present value of debt (% of GNI)	..	33.5	..
Total debt service (% of exports of goods, services and income)	8.2	15.8	..
Official development assistance and official aid (current US$)	173.7 million	6.4 billion	..
Workers' remittances and compensation of employees, received (US$)	1.4 billion	3.3 billion	..

Source: ***World Development Indicators database*, April 2007**

Bibliography

Arbuckle, Gerald, A. <u>Violence, Society, and the Church</u> Collegeville, Minnesota: Liturgical Press, 2004.

Cone, James. <u>God of the Oppressed</u> Mary knoll, New York: Orbis Books, 2003.

Crittenden, Jack. <u>Democracy's Midwife: An Education in Deliberation.</u> Lanham, MD: Lexington Books, 2002.

Deberri, Edward P., and James E. Hug, et al. <u>Catholic Social Teaching: Our Best kept Secret.</u> Maryknoll, NY: Orbis Books, 2003.

Elsbernd, Mary, and Reimund, Bieringer. <u>When Love is not Enough.</u> Collegeville, Minnesota: The Liturgical Press, 2002.

Evans Christopher, editor. <u>The Social Gospel Today</u>. London: Westminster/John Knox Press, 2001.

Freire, Paulo. <u>Pedagogy of the Oppressed</u>. New York: The Continuum International Publishing Group, Inc. 2000.

Gutierrez, Gustavo. <u>A Theology of Liberation 15th Anniversary Edition</u>. MaryKnoll, New York: Orbis Books, 1988.

Hessel, Dieter, T. <u>Social Ministry</u> Revised Edition, Louisville, Kentucky: Westminster/John Knox Press, 1992.

Holland, Joe, and Peter, Henriot. <u>Social Analysis Linking Faith and Justice</u> Washington DC: Dove Communications and Orbis Books, 2004.

Maathai, Wangari. <u>Developing Anti Corruption Strategies in a Changing World: Global Challenges to Civil Society</u>. www.

Transparency.org / 9th international Anti-corruption conference, The Papers

Meredith, Martin. The Fate of Africa, From the Hopes of Freedom to the Hearts of Despair: A History of 50 Years of Independence. New York: Public Affairs, 2005.

Ovienloba, Andrew, editor. The Social Crusade: Thoughts and Reflection. Benin City, Nigeria: Allen's Prints, 2004.

_____. Democracy and Human Rights in Nigeria: Issues and Perspectives. Benin City, Nigeria: Allen's Prints, 2002.

Ratzinger, Joseph Cardinal. God and the World: a Conversation with Peter Seewald. San Francisco: Ignatius Press 2002.

Sachs, Jeffery, D. The End of Poverty: Economic Possibilities for our Time. New York: Penguin Press, 2005.

Schineller, Peter, ed. *The* Voice of the Voiceless: Pastoral Letters and Communiqués of the Catholic Bishop's Conference of Nigeria. Ibadan, Nigeria: Daily Graphics Nig Ltd., 2002.

Sirico, Robert (Rev.) and Rev. Maciej Zieba, editors. The Social Agenda of the Catholic Church: the Magisterial Texts. London: Burns and Oats, 2000.

Stephen Wright, Nigeria: Struggle for Stability and Status , Boulder, CO: Westview Press, 1998.

Sudharshan, Canagarajah, et al. Nigeria-Poverty Assessment: The Evolution of Poverty and Welfare in Nigeria 1985-1995. Washington DC: World Bank, July 19,

1995.

Wink, Walter, editor. <u>Peace is the Way: Writings on Nonviolence from the Fellowship of Reconciliation</u>. MaryKnoll, New York: Orbis Books, 2000

Ecclesiastical Documents on Justice

Austin Flennary, editor. <u>The Documents of the Second Vatican Council vol.1</u> CD ROM Edition. New York: Paulist Press, 1988.

——————— Pastoral Constitution on the Church in the Modern World (Gaudium ET Spes) Vatican Council II, 1965.

Episcopal Conference of Africa and Madagascar (SECAM). *"Justice and Evangelization in Africa",* 1981.

John XXIII, Pope. <u>Mother and Teacher, 1961</u>. Harmony Media, CD ROM Edition

John Paul II, Pope. <u> The Social Concerns of the Church </u>(Sollicitudo Rei Socialis). 1987

Leo XIII, Pope. <u>Rerum Novarum (On the Condition of Labor), 1891</u>. Harmony Media CD ROM Edition

Paul VI, Pope. <u>Octogesim Adveniens</u> <u>A Call to Action, 1971</u>. Harmony Media CD ROM Edition

The Roman Missile, (The Sacramento). New York: Catholic Book Publishing Co.
1985.

The Catechism of the Catholic Church. Paulist Press, CD ROM Edition

United States Catholic Bishops Conference, "Communities of Salt and Light." See www.osjspm.org

United States Catholic Bishops." Economic Justice for All" Pastoral Letter on Catholic Social Teaching and the US Economy.

World Synod of Bishops, Roman Catholic Church. *"Justice in the World"*. 1971.

Encyclopedia/ Internet Resources

Nigerian Oil, Curse of the Black Gold:Hope and Betrayal in the Niger Delta, National Geographic Magazine, February 2007

The Encyclopedia of Catholic Doctrine. Huntington, Indiana; Our Sunday Visitor Publishing Division, Our Sunday Inc. CD ROM Edition 1997

Microsoft® Encarta® Reference Library 2002. © 1993-2001 Microsoft Corporation. All rights reserved.

www.AllAfrica.com

www.CatholicReliefServices (CRS)

www.osjspm.org

www.Transparencyinternational.org

www.vaticannews.com

www.vanguardngr.com/2002/1118072006.html

www.ingramcontent.com/pod-product-compliance
Lightning Source LLC
Chambersburg PA
CBHW020708270326
41928CB00005B/327